RENTING PROPERTY

Ian Muir

SMART STUDENT GUIDES - RENTING PROPERTY

WHAT OTHER PEOPLE ARE SAYING ABOUT 'RENTING PROPERTY'

I particularly liked the detailed checklists, which are very helpful for students researching and preparing to move to the UK.

I hope that every student and parent gets hold of a copy of this book. It's full of gems of advice, which will help every reader (whether they are a student, parent or a more mature tenant) to save money and reduce their potential grief.

I certainly wish I'd had access to some of the practical tips and time/money-saving advice when I was renting properties in the wilds of Portsmouth and London as a student.

Keep the book close because it's a great reference for renting property!

**David Jones, BA (Hons), PG Dip, Dip RSA TEFLA -
Language College Manager**

After many years spent working with young people, I became aware of the problems students face when renting accommodation. Every student should buy this book and keep it by their bedside. It's a goldmine of practical advice that will save them money and make their lives more comfortable.

**Daniel Britton, author 'The Financial Fairy Tales' series
and founder of 'The Personal Finance Academy'**

In this book, Ian Muir displays his great depth of understanding of the student rental market in common and understandable terms. I also appreciated the friendliness of his tone, which made the information appear less intimidating.

Jack Blanchard, graduated two years ago

I liked the bullet point format, which made Ian's book easy to read and dip into when searching for a particular bit of information.

The book also covers everything in good detail – it's not too lengthy but there's enough there so that nothing is missing.

Michael Faulkner, student

Although I rent out properties myself, this book provides scores of additional tips that I know my daughter will benefit from when she goes to university next year.

Eve Risbridger, Environmental Officer

Ian asked me to review this book because both my children recently rented property whilst at university. All I can say is that I wish it had been published before they went! They would have benefited from so much of the advice and personally I am so much clearer regarding how to handle agents and landlords. I understand what their responsibilities are and what is fair. It really would have saved time and money, as well as helping us to be more assertive about issues. This book's an excellent investment.

Lou Sutton, Housewife and mother of university students

With pragmatism, a slice of empathy and a twist of hashtag #wit:-), Ian has managed to blend a cocktail of worthy information that will not only be a useful read, but will also provide a practical tool of knowledge to anyone entering the student rental marketplace.

As a BA Hons 'Architectural Technologist with Interior Design,' I know that there are many rogues in the property industry. I will ensure that my eldest also reads the book before she goes to university this year and will purchase Ian's future editions when my son does.

Rachel Emily Reid, Architectural Technologist & Landlady

This book contains lots of practical advice for students at the time when they most need help. It's also excellent for parents who inevitably end up footing the bill!

Andrew Worth, IT Developer

Dedication

To my lovely daughter, Jillian.
I hope this book has a positive impact on young tenants' lives.
This book would not have happened without your smiles and
happiness when I refurbished your bathroom some
20 years ago, which set me off on a property journey...

I love you more than I've ever told you.

FOREWORD

I first met Ian at a social event I organise for sports and GT car owners. At the time he was based in Bournemouth. In the course of introducing himself to the group, Ian mentioned he was a property refurbisher and landlord and had just written a book for students providing advice on renting property in the UK. My own principal business is managing a language college for international students, so I was naturally interested in the contents of his book. A large number of our students find their own accommodation and some of them are exploited by unscrupulous landlords.

We not only shared an interest in cars and travel, but our businesses intersected at the point of helping students. We arranged to meet and I discovered Ian was not only passionate about assisting students when they are renting property, but he also wanted to help anyone avoid common financial mistakes, a number of which he said he has made himself, despite his knowledge of finance and negotiation. He is also keen on changing education to increase the focus towards the future economy of the UK. On this topic he had some strong but common sense opinions, and I hope that he finds time to get involved in education and to provide additional help for students as they transition into their working lives.

The section of Ian's book that had been written for international students was obviously of interest to me and he asked me to sense-check the contents. I was impressed, as all of the key issues were included and I recognised some of the scenarios my students had faced. I particularly liked the detailed checklists, which are very helpful for students researching and preparing to move to the UK.

In fact, the whole manuscript covered more issues than I would have come up with myself. I was so confident that it would benefit any student renting a property or room that I offered to write an introduction.

Well, here we are four years later and I'm really pleased to see that Ian has at last found time away from his business to complete the book and prepare it for publishing. I'm also delighted that he has given me the opportunity to write this introduction.

I hope that every student and parent gets hold of a copy of this book. It's full of gems that will help every reader – whether they are a student, parent or indeed a more mature tenant – save money and avoid pitfalls.

I certainly wish I'd had access to some of the practical tips and time/money-saving advice when I was renting properties in the wilds of Portsmouth and London as a student.

Keep the book close because it's a great reference for renting property!

David Jones, BA (Hons), PG Dip, Dip RSA TEFLA

Principal and Marketing Director, ETC International College, Bournemouth

CONTENTS

INTRODUCTION

One hundred and forty-seven tips to save money, protect yourself and get your deposit refunded may sound a lot, but I can tell you there are actually a lot more than 147! I lost count around the halfway mark. But I like the number 147. It's the left-hand column of a computer's numeric keyboard – if only I could have managed 741! Coincidentally, I recently read an article by the digital marketing expert Ryan Deiss. He says that the daily number of emails that the average adult receives is 147. That is a good target to reduce my inbox to. One hundred and forty-seven is also the maximum break in snooker. I would like this book to maximise your savings and for you to snooker those who 'try it on'. #smugpun.

I did think of the number 42, as the parents of students will recall that in '*The Hitchhiker's Guide to the Galaxy*', 42 was the answer to the ultimate question of life, the universe and everything. However, in terms of numbers, it would have been massively underselling what you will be getting from this reference book.

Moving on to the content, how many undergraduates do you think there are in the UK? According to HESA (the Higher Education Statistics Agency), there were over 1.7 million in 2014/15. Wow!

Think about how many of those you know who have said their landlord quickly fixed all the problems and:

a)   The agent made no additional charges above the monthly rent.

b)   Their accommodation was as good as living at home.

c)   They got their deposit returned in full.

I bet your answer was less than...er, one.

There are a lot of dissatisfied students out there, but it's easy to criticise and maybe a lot of that is because low standards of accommodation have historically been expected. The accepted explanation is that this is part and parcel of being a student. You may have heard your parents on a Monty Python rant along the lines of, "You're lucky because we used to live in one room, all one hundred and twenty-six of us, with no furniture. Half the floor was missing and we all huddled together in one corner for fear of falling!"

Successful investors, whose inside knowledge invariably leads them to make the right decisions before the herd, often refer to the "smart money". Smart money investors even take what may appear to be contrarian positions on the direction of the market. Throughout this book, I will mention this concept of being SMART in relation to renting.

There are many misunderstandings and potential pitfalls in renting a property. Invariably, students and ultimately their parents, the owners of The Bank of Mum and Dad (BMD), end up with much higher expenditure than they anticipated.

So, this book aims to raise your expectations and provide you with inside knowledge and insight based upon my many years of commercial experience. You will be able to take SMART actions to save time, energy and your money (and your parents' money).

This will be more than a light-bulb moment. It will be like having an LED floodlight; lots of power with low running costs.

So, *why have I written this book*? There are a few reasons, so a bit of background will help explain them.

A couple of decades ago, I was a trainer working for various corporations. For a couple of years, I trained estate agents (for which I still get blamed!). Sadly, the 'peerless' content was similar to the get fit programmes that start in January only to be abandoned by February. I am also a qualified cricket coach. My key skill as a player was in identifying opponents' strengths and weaknesses, although I was less successful at sorting out my own technical deficiencies! (I needed a coach.) So, in business and in sport, I love finding ways to make improvements and helping others to find a better or quicker way to get from A to Z.

Learning the hard way at the 'university of life' is fulfilling but it's also painful, time-consuming and expensive, especially in property. This book pulls together my knowledge from working in the finance and estate agency industry, from being a coach and, more generally, from possessing a lifelong love of identifying ways to improve.

I have been a landlord and refurbisher for over 13 years and my kids have also gone to university and rented their accommodation. Through this I have learnt that many properties are sub-standard.

Within the property industry, I hear of countless instances of tenants being taken advantage of. However, I also hear of scores of incidents of landlords' properties suffering from damage and neglect from tenants who are unaware of or ignore their responsibilities.

I want to shake a few trees and see the private rented sector improve so it becomes fairer to tenants *and* landlords. Life is then more civilised. The government has tried to do this through legislation, but whilst this is well intentioned, the law of unintended consequences applies because it does not understand the marketplace and its actions will result in higher rents, which is the opposite of what was intended. It will also fail to prevent the rogues from operating.

You may be surprised to read that the legal system invariably favours tenants and is stacked against landlords. This is not me talking from a landlord's biased position. Councils and Citizens Advice have been known to give what I believe is immoral advice to tenants regarding how to game the system and stay in a property without paying rent!

There are references to some contractual documentation and legislation within this book that help to explain how to handle specific issues. I have to emphasise that these refer to the law in England and Wales. The laws and relevant statutes in Scotland are different and rather than place references to Scotland at each appropriate point and slow the flow of the book, I have added a separate section at the back, in Appendix 1. This describes the legal position in Scotland (as it was when I first wrote the book in 2013).

Please be aware that there have been some changes in legislation since then, mostly to the benefit of tenants. So that I can more quickly publish the book, at this stage I will say that if you need to know the current legal position then please do your own research rather than rely on what may be outdated legislation quoted in this (or indeed any) book.

How to Use This Book

I hope this book proves to be your *best resource* for saving money whilst renting accommodation, not just for the time you are at university, but for any time you will be renting.

So, in the tradition of a parent I will offer some paternal and patronising advice. In the tradition of a student, you may choose to ignore it. The book is packed full of tips, some of which will immediately save you time or money. Some may help you in a couple of years' time. So, I would strongly recommend that you use the book as a reference. Read the contents page to quickly identify the items of specific interest. Alternatively, if you are reading this electronically, click on the hyperlinks to take you to the chapters that most appeal to you.

When reading the book, keep a highlighter pen handy and use it to mark-up points that you think are actionable. This will make it a much quicker personal reference.

You will see that I have emphasised **SMART** throughout the book. Well, apart from it being appropriate for anyone who has reached university, I like puns. **SMART**, in this case, is also an acronym for **S**tudents **M**oney-Saving **A**nd **R**ental **T**ip. However, if you like a word challenge and would like a mention in any future updates, please email me at im@smartstudentguides.com with any alternative (and polite) meanings for the acronym SMART.

 SMART tips are highlighted with a 'SMART' light bulb. This will help you identify the immediate opportunities for savings and 'disadvantageous' and, in some instances, illegal practices, enabling you to manage problems before, during and after the tenancy.

 In addition, there are checklists and valuable additional information that you can download from the website, so please log onto **www.smartstudentguides.com/bookdocs** I have also provided useful websites that will be of benefit, as the information and legislation is regularly changing, so use the search terms I've suggested to find the current information.

It's now time to GOWI (Get On With It, or GerrOnWiyIt, as my Yorkshire cousins would spell it.)

CHAPTER ONE

Rental Market Overview

This chapter will give you some insight into being a landlord and the responsibilities involved. By helping you understand landlords, you will be able to manage them more effectively and be more confident. A good relationship will invariably result in a more amenable landlord, which means less hassle, lower costs and more comfortable accommodation, as they will be more inclined to attend to problems that you have highlighted.

In the UK, we love to own property. It's part of our culture and 'getting on the property ladder' is a bit of a national obsession. Before the 2008 banking crisis, I read that the only nation with a higher proportion of owners-to-renters was Ireland.

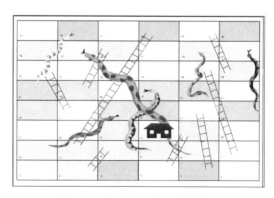

Figure 1 - Property snakes and ladders

Our obsession with property is fuelled by the media continually stating percentage rises in house prices, and on TV they regularly show how much money even the cheerfully naïve 'investor' can make. With the historically low interest rates currently being offered on mortgages, people are under the impression that they can make easy profits from investing in properties. Of course, this is not the whole story.

According to the economics website www.primeeconomics.org, the average national house price has risen over the past 20 years from £62,333 to £247,000. This is a 296% increase in value. By comparison, inflation has grown less than 4% per annum, which when compounded over those years equals approximately 140%. This is a very healthy above inflation growth for an investor. However, past performance is no guarantee of future returns.

Many people have recently invested in property because they have been frustrated by the pitiful interest rates offered by banks and underwhelmed by pension and stock market fund performances.

However, buying, maintaining, renting and selling property can be extremely expensive, and many landlords have been surprised to see their margins (the difference between their mortgage and the rent received) eroded by a long list of unexpected costs.

Investing in property rentals used to be about rental income over the long term, but with recent house price inflation, it often costs so much to buy a property that the rent achieved barely covers the cost of the mortgage. Landlords are therefore relying on capital growth to achieve a return on their investment. This is very risky as interest rates could rise and the rental market may not be able to pay higher rents.

This is not healthy for the private rented sector and therefore for tenants in particular. Being a landlord is a socially important role that needs responsible, long-term thinking, planning and action.

As a result of the very high costs of managing and maintaining a property, many new (and uninformed) landlords will discover when they prepare their annual accounts and pay tax that they are actually losing money. This will increase dramatically over the next couple of years thanks to the government's (astonishingly inept and unfair) introduction of new tax changes that are targeted at landlords, many of whom still don't understand the implications of these changes.

This means many landlords will be looking to save costs and reduce repairs. This will adversely affect you as a tenant!

At this stage then, it's worth explaining some of the financial issues of being a landlord. It may give you a very useful insight into aspects of the business should you want to start your own one at some stage in the future.

Income from property rentals is usually perceived as the difference between what a landlord pays for their mortgage and the rent they receive from tenants. That can appear to be very healthy. Unfortunately, many property investors still get blinded by this attractive but inaccurate headline 'profit'.

The issue is that this is *gross* profit. It is a mistake for anyone to look at this simple calculation. *Net* profit is what is important, and it's what remains after costs are also deducted.

In property business, the costs are substantial. They include:

→ The cost of repairs to the building to make it habitable and legally compliant.

→ The cost of repairs to furnishings and fittings, e.g. washing machines, boilers, plumbing, WAT (Wear And Tear).

→ Agency fees.

→ Compliance and certification.

→ Administration.

→ The landlord's own time (which has a £ per hour value).

→ Business overheads.

→ Council tax, which has to be paid even if there are no tenants.

→ The biggest worry - void periods, i.e. when the property doesn't have any tenants, which for a landlord in the student marketplace is likely to be for two months per year (a 17% reduction in revenue).

If, after all these costs a landlord makes any profit, they have HM Revenue and Customs chasing them for income tax and/or capital gains tax.

In many parts of the country, notably in the more expensive South East, these net costs are now in excess of the profit. Many investors are relying on property price increases for their profit. Very risky!

Students usually rent rooms in Houses of Multiple Occupation (HMOs). These potentially offer the investor/landlord a higher return on their money as a result of the number of rooms that *can* be rented within a property.

HMOs have a lot of additional responsibilities and legislation that need to be complied with. However, property-related legislation is cumbersome, frequently open to interpretation and in many cases misunderstood. Therefore, it may be inadvertently bypassed even by those with the best intentions.

Many investors really don't understand the rental market. It is very time-consuming and frustrating managing properties and people, as well as understanding legislation. It is a 24/7/365 responsibility, which is why many delegate the job to agents, which is a big expense. This is not to say their fees are unreasonable, as it's a labour-intensive and time-pressured job.

To give you an understanding of the responsibilities of a landlord or agent, have a read through the following ones:

→ Deposits to manage and register.

→ Ongoing repairs.

→ Agents and tradesmen to manage, as well as arranging convenient times to gain access.

→ Gas certificates.

→ HMO compliance.

→ HSE (Health and Safety) compliance, which now includes risk assessments.

→ Changing legislation.

→ Adverts to place and reply to.

→ New tenants to find, meet and reference.

→ Non-payment of rent.

→ Legislation that protects bad tenants makes it very difficult to remove them. Authorities, Citizens Advice and councils give advice to tenants regarding how to remain in a property even when they aren't paying rent. There may, therefore, be court cases, which can drag on for several months and are extremely time-consuming and stressful.

→ Mortgage payments.

→ Compliance with council demands and their sometimes politically-motivated misinterpretation of legislation.

→ Complaints from neighbours (I had to cut down a tree because it was blocking the sun from a neighbour's patio – the logistics of this were challenging and involved renting cutting equipment, climbing up a tree, trying to get parents to control their children and transporting branches through the house and off to the recycling centre.)

→ Complaints about rubbish, parking, noise and ASB (Anti-Social Behaviour).

→ Repairs to the building and planning future repair and redecoration schedules.

→ Tenants' demands to fix things when it's simply the case they don't know how to operate a switch or have lost their keys.

→ Tenants' financial problems (you have to sit and listen, but many stories are simply excuses).

→ Tenants damaging a property, sometimes maliciously.

→ Understanding housing benefits and how to help tenants complete documents is very complex and needs a separate book (it's not my marketplace as I see it as too time-consuming to try and understand and manage). Net profit is low (and that's assuming an interest only mortgage - using a repayment mortgage means there is virtually no profit!). Financial risk and keeping up-to-date with the mortgage and commercial lending marketplace.

→ Taxation and preparing annual accounts (probably as much fun as pushing needles under your toenails). You have to keep up-to-date on accounting issues. As an example, a few years ago I had to inform my accountant about a taxation issue that would enable me to reclaim expenditure on foreign property I was renting out (and they tried to charge me for researching this). A couple of years later the accountants had to educate HMRC on the same issue, as they were short-staffed. If they hadn't I would have paid far too much tax.

→ Fitting *all this* in and around a day job.

In short, it's a lot more difficult to be a landlord than people imagine, so it's a shock to most new ones who have believed the media hype that buy-to-let is a guaranteed way to secure their financial future. All tenants see is the amount of rent they are paying each week or month to the landlord. They think this is all profit, with the landlord doing next to nothing on their behalf. However, return on investment is a topic for landlords.

A landlord's responsibilities are 24/7/365, so even going on holiday can be a big worry, unless they are prepared to pay for a letting agent to provide a fully-managed service. A good letting agent is hard to find and sadly some are little more than form-fillers and rent collectors. Agents normally charge approximately 15% of the rent, which is more than the net profit some landlords are making. Hence, many landlords can't afford to use agencies for the management of their properties.

However, statistics show that most landlords only have one property that they rent out, and if they have a full-time job that's not necessarily near the said property. This is when agencies are more likely to be used.

Unfortunately, as many landlords are inexperienced, and some agents don't provide a service that cares for tenants, many landlord obligations are not fulfilled. As a result, un-SMART students who don't understand these obligations are at a big disadvantage.

A crusty, experienced landlord will more than likely be a cynic. If they have numerous properties at the low end of the rental market, e.g. housing benefit tenants, then they will have had innumerable bad experiences of tenants not paying but also damaging their property, and of disruptive tenants who upset or cheat other tenants. They will have been frequently lied to and had to take some tenants to court. As a result, they will not trust anyone or believe a word a tenant says.

We had a lovely new executive apartment in Hove that was rented to a couple plus their male friend. Having been reliable for the first seven or eight months, a payment didn't arrive. The man, who owned bars and a nightclub, got a message to us that the lady we thought was his 'life partner' (it subsequently turns out she wasn't and the other bloke was his boyfriend...) had been 'put into an institution' and he had been involved in a hold-up involving guns. He provided an article from the local press for proof.

There was a report of such an incident, which was a bit of a worry. However, in chasing him by email, he replied he was no longer allowed by the police to communicate because his assailants were still after him and he had been put into a 'safe house'. Er, that means not communicating by email either?

You have to admire people's creativity, which is easier to do when the large deposit covers your loss of rent.

Examples like this should give you an idea why landlords are cynical by nature. Where money is involved, people's morals can fall down a crevasse.

So bear in mind that some landlords will automatically blame tenants, and in the case of students will probably assume you are lazy (students tend to stay in bed late), untidy (don't pretend) and have a life of partying, etc. (this I don't believe ☺).

Nevertheless, they still have responsibilities and you need them to respond and treat you *fairly* and *lawfully*.

The better landlords will also be members of a recognised organisation, such as the National Landlords Association (www.landlords.org.uk/), which is the largest and the one I belong to, the Residential Landlords Association (www.rla.org.uk/), or any number of local associations based around the country.

Standards of accommodation are improving, as there is more competition for landlords to find tenants. This is resulting in more investment into rental properties so they're cleaner, more modern, better equipped, have better decor, more double beds rather than single ones, more kitchen space, desks, broadband, flat-screen TVs, etc. Basically, the accommodation is more suited to the needs of students rather than desperate boarders.

The better news for students is that they are now in a stronger negotiating position than their predecessors.

Landlords who don't update their properties will have void periods. These are painful, especially so in the student marketplace because if the landlord doesn't find tenants before the start of the academic year they can be faced with several months without rent.

If they are to make any money, it's *essential* for landlords to have paying tenants. Where local demand for rooms has reduced, or there is an oversupply of rooms to rent, a landlord who has vacant rooms will be worried. This is an opportunity for you to negotiate lower rental payments.

CHAPTER TWO

Letting Agents

I've just attended a conference and one of the presentations was by David Hyner on goal setting (look him up on Google or YouTube). He has a great story in which he talks about *'going rhino'*, which is effectively charging through problems. It brought me back to when I trained estate agents and we referred to them as rhinos because they were thick skinned, short-sighted and charged a lot!

Figure 2 - An agent can be thick skinned,
short-sighted and charge a lot

Letting agents also have a difficult job. They have time pressures, especially the ones who operate in the student marketplace where they have to deal with sharers, many of whom have no experience of looking after property. This means they have to spend a lot of time 'nannying'.

Some of the problems in the rental marketplace are as a result of there being no regulation, no qualifications or indeed any prior experience or skill needed to set up an agency. The only requirements are determination, some interpersonal skills, a few contacts, an ability to act quickly and an eye for an opportunity.

However, remember that agents are paid by landlords, so their duty is to their clients. They are certainly not all vultures picking at the bones. There are some outstandingly good letting agents out there who not only have service-level agreements with landlords, but will refuse to have them as a client (or 'sack' them) if the landlord doesn't achieve those standards. They will even take a paternal interest in their students because by doing this they will have fewer time-wasting issues to manage.

Good agents will always be busy, which is why you need to have a degree of empathy and understand that not all your issues will be at the top of their priority list. Later on I will highlight a couple of examples.

For now though, I'll provide a bit more background so you can understand how the market works and what you need to do to make it work better for you.

The costs to start-up a letting agency business are very low. Also, unlike an estate agent who needs a high street location, a letting agent can successfully operate from shared premises or even from their bedroom.

With low start-up costs, an increasing demand for rental properties and low overheads, it's easy for someone with an entrepreneurial outlook to get up and running. There are no compliance issues and they'll be dealing with a client base of investor landlords and tenants who will be predominantly inexperienced and won't demand the level of service that should be expected.

It's also very easy for estate agents to enter the rental market, because they already have the high street presence and fixed overheads. All they need to do is add another desk and member of staff and start marketing. However, property rentals is a very different marketplace and involves different skills.

So, we find the marketplace you are searching includes a fairly large number of opportunistic 'profit-maximisers' (and maxi misers) looking for easy profits and no expenditure. There is nothing wrong with the principle of making profit, as long as the customer knows what they are paying for, and what they should be receiving in return. However, some of the tactics in the industry are underhand, so I want to prepare you. #smartstudent.

By asking them a couple of questions, you can assess an agent quite quickly.

1. **Ask which property redress scheme they belong to (as this is a legal requirement).**

   If they are not members of a property redress scheme don't rent from them because they are operating unlawfully.

   Their membership of a property redress scheme will give you a simple route to redress, should they let you down in any way and, in particular, if they do not provide the property/service that was agreed and which should be part of your contract (AST).

2. **Ask the agent when the last time they 'fired' a landlord was, or refused to rent a landlord's properties, and what the reasons for this were.** A good agent will have done this because they will be selective of their clients and won't want to have properties from disreputable landlords on their books because it's bad for their image.

Figure 3 - Agents have been described as behaving as if it's the Wild West

Letting Agency Fees

When renting through an agent, in order to provide you with greater security of any payments and transparency regarding their fees, **I recommend you rent through an agent who is affiliated with a professional body,** as they set standards that agents must adhere to. If they are not a member of one, ask why and evaluate their reasons.

It's therefore best that you choose agents who are members of the following organisations:

- ✓ Association of Residential Letting Agents (ARLA)
- ✓ National Association of Estate Agents (NAEA)
- ✓ Royal Institution of Chartered Surveyors (RICS)
- ✓ National Association of Valuers and Auctioneers (NAVA)

ARLA, NAEA and NAVA are now all connected and are setting agreed standards, although historically ARLA has been for rental agencies, with the others being more frequently seen in estate agencies that may now have expanded into the rental marketplace.

In addition to these organisations, the National Approved Letting Scheme (NALS) is an independent licensing scheme for the accreditation of letting agents.

However, I have heard of agents who have fraudulently claimed membership, so I suggest that where the agent has been in the town less than a year, ask for their membership number and then check via the internet or make a quick phone call to the organisation in order to verify their membership.

The Advertising Standards Authority is also looking to ensure that agents disclose their 'relevant fees' within their adverts, although in his 2016 Autumn statement, the Chancellor announced that letting agent fees were to be banned. When this will become legislation and in what form has yet to be finalised. Mostly this ban on fees will be good for tenants, but some will ultimately mean that rents will increase. One would hope that the government will take advice from consumer groups such as Shelter *and* professional organisations such as the National Landlords Association to ensure the new rules are fair and not ambiguous. Personally, I am sceptical but look forward to the government surprising me. In the meantime, we just have to work with the rules as they stand.

Others

You may come across a situation where the person offering the property for rent is not the landlord or the agent. This doesn't happen very often, but the frequency of these incidents will increase because there are landlords who want to avoid the day-to-day hassles and fear of void periods (the property is empty and no rent is being paid). Rather than sell, however, they lease their property to an 'investor', who effectively becomes the manager by paying the landlord a rent for the property and subletting the rooms to students. This type of arrangement is known as Rent to Rent, R2R, Rent to Let, or variations of these names.

Many of these R2R managers refer to themselves as landlords, but they don't have a lot of experience (it's a scheme that has only really been in operation since 2012). This means their paperwork can be a little bit less than thorough, and they may not have a comprehensive legal agreement in place with the owner that defines who is responsible for repairs, council tax and utilities, etc. It is also unclear if the owner's mortgage and insurance company have agreed to such an arrangement or what happens if the owner fails to pay their mortgage or the manager fails to pay the owner.

In addition, although it's not a widespread problem, be aware that there have been recent instances where people have rented out properties they don't even own, which can be done if the owner of an empty property has been untraceable for a few years.

 All you have to do is ask for **proof of identity** (agents are supposed to do this) and a **copy of their previous month's council tax and utility bills**. Also, quickly check via Land Registry to find out the property owner's name. Currently it will cost you £3 to do this. **www.landregistry.gov.uk/public/property-ownership**

CHAPTER THREE

Leaving Home

Figure 4 - Taking flight from the nest

Leaving the nest for the first time?

Well, the following is not on the same level of risk as a student leaving home…it's more like taking your life into your hands by going to a Millwall football match in the 1990s, but do watch this lovely and dramatic clip: Chicks Jump Off Cliff – Life Story – BBC www.youtube.com/watch?v=JkBSkFyUyv0

When leaving the comfort of your parents' home, irrespective of whether you are a fresher or second year student, if you want a softer landing then you need to **start looking for your accommodation early in order to snag yourself a better property.**

The longer you wait to do your research, the bigger the rush to find good accommodation will be and the less choice you will have. If you wait, you may miss the better-quality options...

Freshers are usually able to find accommodation on campus, but not always, so it's important to be prepared.

As every parent knows, students are fully capable of providing fine-dining plus wine on a budget of £3 per day, fixing plumbing leaks and out-manoeuvring streetwise jackals. They don't need Google because they know it all. They are bloody smart-arses, so they don't ask their parents for advice. Even when the parents are landlords... Sarcasm aside, I've sat at the end of a phone in frustration listening to the complaint about rats. "Aaaarrggghhhh, you eejut," I've said. "Didn't we tell you not to rent that hovel?!!!" So, my advice is to think early to anticipate problems and question the people who are most likely to know. Tip: it won't be your mates. End of paternal rant.

According to agents, one of the issues that causes the most problems is that students don't worry enough about their choice of property and with whom they will be sharing. You really don't want to be living in a nice house that becomes a pigsty because your new mates don't clean up after themselves and expect someone else, i.e. you, to be their surrogate mum.

Also consider how you will deal with the person who does not want to pay his/her share of the utility, food bills, etc. Your new best friend might be a poor money-manager and this will be very stressful for you.

It's therefore vitally important that you discuss and agree these issues *before* you start house hunting.

So, in looking for accommodation, don't assume everything will be ok. Tomorrow may be too late, as the best and most convenient accommodation will have been taken. So, if you want to snag yourself one of the best properties, GOWI!

Another issue highlighted by agents is that students transform from being passive and uninterested about finding a property into being in a state of panic when they actually start looking. As a result, many students agree to take a room in an unacceptable state with an unacceptable contract and with the wrong housemates.

Be warned - it is costly to change mid-contract!!!

The SMART student gets organised early.

In my old area, Bournemouth, where there is a very big student population and a well-established rental market, the agents regularly tried to persuade students to find their accommodation in October for the following year. This is beyond advanced planning. I've spoken to agents in the large university towns of Durham and Nottingham and it's similar there. Apparently, there is a lemming-like rush to find somewhere before Xmas. However, there are usually plenty of properties available in January so any pre-Christmas panic seems to be as a result of word on the street rather than a reality of the marketplace.

Speak to your Students' Union to get their opinion regarding the usual level of property availability.

Having a realistic idea of your timeframe is a good start. You'll then know when to start looking in order to avoid the rush. Ensure you have done enough research and found suitable housemates, and don't sign up to anything because you feel rushed. **In fact, never sign a contract**

you don't fully understand. Get advice. It's better to miss out on a property than to sign an onerous contract. Be patient. In Nottingham, for instance, in mid-2016, there was a 12% over-supply of properties. So if this is the case, there will be many landlords who will be very worried that they won't find tenants, which would be very financially painful. That's great for negotiating down the rent or asking for the provision of additional services, repairs or replacements (which you will need to get in writing before you sign a contract)!

It isn't only students who make the mistake of signing up to things without checking the finer details. I've heard from agents that many parents also sign up to contracts in a rush. They frequently assume they are only responsible for the rent of their beloved teenager for the duration of the term and forget the contract covers an entire year. If they end up paying for five other students as well it can be very costly.

Location

 To save time, energy and travel costs, I recommend that you get a map of the area, even if it's just a printout of a Google Map. You can make notes on it when you start asking for advice. Check out Google Earth too!

For information on the different areas within a town or city, it's really worth *investing the time to do the research*.

Initially, speak with the Students' Union, as they will be **familiar with the areas students prefer and why**. Ask them about the local rental rates. Bear in mind that as a result of supply and demand, some universities may have fewer students attending that year, or more properties available for rent, especially as a number of councils are building their own student accommodation. This results in more accommodation being available than there is demand for that accommodation. As I mentioned earlier, landlords could get desperate so you can negotiate for lower rents.

Also, ask for their advice on the areas, letting agents and landlords to avoid, and why. Grill the postgrads you know too. They usually know the area well and will have a more settled social life, so they are more likely to avoid staying in the typical student areas but will have knowledge of the good, the bad and the ugly. You could try a Google search for "problems in X area". If nothing else, you should get information on broadband, utility and traffic problems.

Speak to a couple of letting agents to see what they say. You can search for them using the following websites:

→ www.rightmove.co.uk/estate-agents.html/svr/1711

→ www.zoopla.co.uk/find-agents/letting-agents/

Preferably, find an agent who has been in the area for a long time, as their opinion will be more valid. A young agent may not live in the town and may have recently been transferred from another branch. Even if they don't specialise in student lets, ask them to give you the name of an agent who does (it's important to speak to a specialist). National agency chains will have many properties on their books as a result of their brand awareness and marketing campaigns. However, they may have higher staff turnover, so the agents may be younger and less knowledgeable on the market and the area.

A number of landlords will place their own adverts, as they don't use letting agents, so check out these websites for comparisons:

→ www.gumtree.com/flats-and-houses-for-rent

→ www.student.spareroom.co.uk

→ www.accommodationforstudents.com

→ www.studentpad.co.uk

→ Also, a number of smaller landlords in university towns are using www.students.com, so check this out too.

Things you should consider:

✓ Is there a **short travel time** to lectures?

✓ Can you get **into town by rail** (tram in some cities) or bus, or is there a safe route to cycle?

✓ Is the accommodation in **close proximity to a decent supermarket?**

✓ If there isn't a washing machine, does it have **close proximity to a launderette?**

✓ **Are there pubs, bars, fast-food outlets nearby?** (There will be times when they will be needed, we just hope that it won't be every night!)

✓ **Is the property next to anywhere noisy or where you will be disturbed?** E.g. a railway line, above or adjacent to a busy shop(s) or food outlet (smells), in close proximity to a pub, on a main road, near a fuel station, bus stop, sports arena, anywhere that's open late at night or has bright lights on all night, e.g. a factory, or overhead power lines.

Research

To some, researching a new area and place to live is fun. To others it's a chore. However, it's invaluable, so if it's not a task you are likely to have the patience for you may find it easier to get your friends or parents to help with your initial searching and screening.

Start your research by checking out some websites and get an idea of the typical rents being charged and the types of rooms available. You will then need to set a budget.

When looking for your accommodation, **ensure that you are comparing** *total costs*, because similar rooms can vary substantially both in price and in what costs are included.

An increasing number of landlords now offer rent that includes some or all of the utility bills and broadband, or will cap them at a certain cost per month.

Again, I refer you to your Students' Union, who will provide you with some local knowledge. Don't be afraid to ask letting agents for help, as they ultimately want your business, so they should be keen to assist.

Follow this link: **www.smartstudentguides.com/bookdocs** to download a list of websites that are good for searching for rental properties. There are also links to Google Maps and WeGo, the app I use for GPS directions when I'm travelling (I think it's much better than Google's app).

Once a potentially suitable property has been identified, use the most popular property internet portals for agents: Rightmove and Zoopla. Search for the same property to see how many agents are advertising it.

By noting the different agents, it will provide an alternative to:

a)   Arrange a viewing.

b)   Negotiate with another agent to get better terms of business.

When arranging viewings, it's often a better use of time to view a number of properties in a day. You can also then make immediate comparisons between what you have seen. Seeing four to six properties in a day should give you a good scope for comparison and sufficient time to have a good look around the area. Once you have a specific day or alternative days available, it's just a matter of phoning the agents/advertisers and arranging a schedule of visits. Agents are typically available from nine to five Monday to Friday, and some agents or landlords will be happy to arrange viewings outside of normal business hours or on Saturdays or Sundays.

I suggest that only the first and maybe second page of the property details needs to be printed out. It's also helpful to make appropriate notes from your phone call with the agents/advertisers, and take these with you to the viewing.

If using Rightmove, be aware that the phone number that's displayed in the advert is a redirection through them, so it may cost more money. You could save money by opening another browser page and finding the agent's website for its direct phone number.

When visiting the town or city suburb, it's sensible to get a copy of the local paper that includes property adverts. Within this you can look for additional properties that landlords are advertising direct. This can be an excellent money-saver, as you're not paying for the big brands. Savings are not guaranteed and this is not a replacement to educating yourself on the local market, but it's a good way to start.

Students' Union

Your Students' Union can be extremely helpful, not just on property-related matters, so do get in touch with them if there's anything you're not sure about. They do a lot more than manage the union bar and social calendar!

Regarding property, they can provide information and advice on:

✓ Best rental locations.

✓ Types of property and rental rates.

✓ Agents and landlords who are known to them (they will know those with good and bad reputations).

✓ Availability of accommodation and when you need to start looking.

✓ Public transport.

✓ Car parking permit arrangements.

✓ Local knowledge, e.g. nightlife and shopping.

✓ Issues with your landlord or agent.

Housemates

Choosing housemates

Figure 5 - Could this be your housemate? Or you?

Maybe you haven't yet lived with someone who leaves their clothes littered in every room and their dirty plates in the sink, who never does their share of bathroom cleaning, uses your toiletries, snores so loudly that the doors bang and plays Stairway to Heaven on their didgeridoo at 3am every morning.

Did you always get on with your brothers and sisters? How often did you fight? How did things get resolved? It's somewhat trickier with people who are not family. One day you will experience the aggravation, the joy and the occasional horrors of living with other people.

You will spend a substantial amount of your time with your housemates in student accommodation over the course of the year, so it's worthwhile thinking carefully about who you want to share with, rather than just accepting an invitation to join a group.

It's easy to think that as students you will be flexible, as it's all part of the experience. Unfortunately, wisdom teaches you that you don't know someone until you've lived with them, and some seemingly trivial issues can become a major annoyance over a period of time, which means you'll end up arguing or permanently aggravated. You don't need this added stress.

One consistent issue that agents have highlighted to me is that many students form groups too soon and without thought.

Humans are pack animals. There is a natural fear of not belonging to a group. Frequently, students form groups with people they have just met, but after a couple of months they realise they either don't get on or have become part of a different social circle. It also means that the person you enjoy drinking with may not be the person you enjoy living with.

Admittedly, this doesn't sound like much of an issue, but in reality it can be. This is because a tenancy agreement is a legal document and you will be tied to that from the start of the next academic year.

Effectively, being a housemate is an 18-month commitment! Much as we may think we can simply walk away and change, it isn't that simple.

You are committed to paying rent on that property.

Also, if you sign a joint contract you will be held jointly responsible for any damages or losses. This can mean you end up paying for a careless housemate.

If you do want to change, landlords are under no obligation to alter tenancy agreements. However, if you find someone else who is a reputable tenant, a good agent will do what they can to get a swap arranged. Of course, there is likely to be an administration cost for the extra hassle you have caused, but this is better than living somewhere you don't want to be.

So, try to think about what you are like to live with and what will annoy other people. Then think about the issues or characteristics in others that will aggravate you.

Consider what you and your friends will be like with the following:

→ **Trust** – food, sharing costs and housework, handling the landlord and agents and organising socials.

→ **Consideration** – e.g. quietness, sticking to agreements, such as no pets.

→ **Security** – communal doors, windows and bedrooms being entered or doors being left open.

→ **Privacy.**

→ **Tidiness.**

→ **Hours** – early to bed or night owl?

→ **Partying** – the extent, hours, noise level, mess, additional guests.

→ **Smoking** – one or all of your housemates may object to the smell, so how will you manage a smoker, whether tobacco or drugs?

→ **Financial management** – you don't want to be chasing housemates for their share of the bills.

Before signing a rental agreement, you all need to decide how you will handle the payment of bills and also agree that if anyone leaves before the end of the agreement they will still be liable for their share of the costs until a replacement housemate is found, and the responsibility for that should be with the departing housemate.

Best friends

Even if you are the *best of friends*, you may have completely different standards and diametrically-opposed approaches to domestic issues that could make living together so difficult that your friendship comes to an end. Consider whether it would be better for both of you to stay as good friends and live separately.

Relationships

Whether these existed before uni or evolved whilst there, relationships may be best kept *out of shared accommodation*, no matter how well you get on. This is because the relationship may not last as long as your tenancy agreement, which could add financial woes to your emotional ones, which in turn is likely to affect your relationships with your housemates.

As a suggestion, *make a list of the issues you will find unacceptable to live with*, then use these to help you select potential housemates.

CHAPTER FOUR

Viewing

The Viewing

This is more exciting! So, now you've got yourself organised, chosen your top half-dozen properties, printed out the details and found the agents' direct numbers, you will need to agree with your potential housemates how you will make the decisions. Will you all go together? When are you all available? How should the viewing be handled if only one of you can do the initial one?

The objective is to find the most suitable property, not any property. You will need a sense of urgency if a property appears ideal, as it's unlikely to stay on the market for long. You will have a number of options, so to save valuable time give priority to the best properties rather than all those that are available. Conversely, you don't want to only see one property. It's important to physically see a few so you can make comparisons and get a better feel for the property and its area.

Questions to ask before you view

When you phone up to enquire about the availability of a property, it's vital to ask a few key questions so you can make comparisons. It's important to make these on the right criteria so the answers will help you prioritise your viewings or even dismiss some properties altogether.

Asking the right questions may save you a wasted trip.

There's a checklist of questions to ask
on the downloads page of the website
www.smartstudentguides.com/bookdocs

When you've shortlisted a few properties, it can be difficult to arrange viewings on the same day without zig-zagging across town or having big waiting times between viewings. A very useful technique used by successful salespeople, who have to be experts at making appointments, will help. This is called the 'alternative close'.

You need to offer two or more alternative times for a viewing, both of which are convenient for YOU. The landlord or agent who will be taking you around is more likely to agree to a time if they have more than one option and therefore feel in control. For example, first ask whether it would be best to make the appointment in the morning or the afternoon. If it's the latter, tell them you can make 1.15pm or 4.45pm (remember, these will be times convenient for you). By doing it this way, you have subtly directed them, using the 'alternative close' technique twice, and you will be able to fit it around the other viewings that you have (or would like to) set up. Also, there is an implication that by meeting at the quarter hour you will only want to spend 15-minutes at the property. #multiskilledstudent.

Give yourself half an hour for a viewing and use Google Maps to help you approximate the time you'll need to travel to the next property.

Meeting the agent

If you have arranged the viewings through the agent(s), they should accompany you. If not, you'll need to know who you will be meeting. It can be to your advantage if you're going to meet the landlord, as long as you set out to make a good impression!

Agents may be less inclined to do viewings after 6pm or on Sundays, although hours of work are unsurprisingly longer in major cities. There is actually a personal security issue outside of the normal nine to five-thirty working hours, especially at night if the agent hasn't previously met you. Many agents are female and agents' safety became a big issue as a result of the much-publicised incident in 1986, when the estate agent Suzy Lamplugh went missing (see the section on Personal Safety). So don't be too hard on an agent if they won't agree to meet you much beyond office hours.

However, there are circumstances when you may prefer not to be accompanied by an agent, as it gives you the opportunity to meet the owner/landlord and build up a rapport. This definitely works to your advantage if they have met you and you have been cheerful, respectful and they perceive you to be trustworthy.

Some rental agents will try to charge you for a viewing (I have heard of £100). This may be because they have a lot of students who set up viewings and then don't turn up. If they insist on a viewing fee, then I would personally decline the viewing and see if another agent is advertising the property. If you feel that you have no option, ask them why they need the fee and how and when they intend to refund you. At worst, insist on an immediate cash refund if you turn up on time.

In their defence, agents are paid by the landlord to get the property rented, so they are keen to meet with genuinely interested applicants and not have their time wasted, so please respect their time, but don't let them pull a fast one.

Please note that as highlighted earlier in the book, it was announced in late 2016 that new legislation is being introduced whereby agents will no longer be allowed to charge tenant fees, but there is currently no date or a definition regarding which fees will be eliminated.

Sherlocking

Figure 6 - Look closely!

What to look out for...

Sherlocking is my term for doing a bit of vital research by fully inspecting your potential home.

This whole section is mega-important.

So you can print copies, I have included the key points in a Viewing Checklist, which can be found on the website **www.smartstudentguides.com/bookdocs**

However, *this section* of the book gives explanations.

When meeting an agent, **take a document that proves you have the right to rent.** Even if you were born in the UK, you will not be offered a property until you have produced this document. **A full list of acceptable documents can be found at** www.gov.uk/government/publications/right-to-rent-document-checks-a-user-guide. This is an important document and you should not part with it. Take a good photocopy with you so you can give it to the landlord or agent if you decide to rent the property - they have a legal requirement to hold it on their files.

Regarding the following points, I know the first couple are obvious, but despite this, many people still don't abide by them and it puts them at a disadvantage. If this is a nice property, several people are going to want to rent it and the person you are meeting is probably going to influence the decision as to who gets to rent it.

With this in mind you may want to ensure you:

✓ Are on time.

✓ Are polite, neatly dressed.

✓ Ask if you need to remove your shoes before you enter, particularly if the hallway is carpeted.

✓ Ask the agent for a copy of the property details and a copy of the Service Level Agreement they have with their landlords. This is to get an idea if the agent is professional and understands the level of service they are committed to offer. Bonus points for any agent who i) has an SLA ii) thinks to bring a copy with them. However, sadly, most agents do not have SLAs.

✓ Ask to see the HMO licence. Not all HMOs need to be licensed, but you will be able to find out from your local council website which properties do need them. This should actually be on display on the wall of the property, but if it isn't you need to see it. If the property isn't licensed you may be disrupted if this is discovered during the tenancy.

✓ Ask about fire precautions. It is a legal requirement to provide a Means of Escape that gives occupiers 30 minutes to safely exit once a fire has started. Do not be fobbed off. NOTHING is more important than your life and health.

DO NOT rent a property which has not had a Fire Risk Assessment

✓ Ask the agent for details on the broadband connection, supplier and speed.

✓ Ask yourself whether the property feels like a house or a home? The latter is usually because the landlord cares and has made an effort to provide somewhere nice to live.

✓ It's your money (or The Bank of Mum and Dad's money), so don't be shy about asking difficult questions, as it will be harder to ask them later when something may have become an urgent issue.

✓ Don't be concerned if the agent is rushing you to make a decision; it's their job to get the property rented. It may be genuine, but if you feel they are being too pushy just smile and be polite, then tell them you need to discuss it with friends/your parents – you may need the agent at a later date to negotiate better terms with the landlord. Don't ever get aggressive. If you are pressured, think about why they are in such a rush. Perhaps they are having problems renting it? Is there something wrong with the property?

✓ If there are a few of you who are looking to rent together then it's best that you all view potential properties together. Some landlords will not offer you a property unless all the sharers are there at the viewing. The landlord is also likely to be impressed with this level of interest and organisation, and you will all be in a better position to judge and agree on a property.

Now to the specific things to look for:

 Take your viewing checklist with you.
You can download it from:
www.smartstudentguides.com/bookdocs

1. Is the communal area big enough to fit you all in?

2. Are all the bedrooms big enough and do they have enough storage? Bedrooms within a property are usually in a similar state of repair, but size can be an issue if you are looking to rent as a group. If a bedroom is in a worse condition than the others or is only big enough for a single bed, then I suggest agreeing on a different share of the overall rent. Once you have done this you can, if necessary, draw lots for the rooms.

3. Are there enough toilets and showers for all of you to avoid queuing? Do the showers work, and do they produce more than a trickle? Test the temperature control. Is there enough pressure to run two or more showers at the same time? If there are more than four of you sharing, at least one toilet must be in a room separate from the bathroom/shower room.

4. Is there enough parking in the driveway and in the road outside? If not, how easy is it to get permits? Also, where can bicycles be safely stored?

5. Is there a washing machine or, better still, a washer/dryer? You need a decent spin speed to ensure clothes dry quickly and you don't have to dry clothes in your room – a big cause of damp. I would recommend a spin speed of 1400rpm or 1200rpm if the machine is top quality, e.g. Miele or Bosch. Nothing less than 1000rpm. If there is no washing machine, life will be very difficult so you will ideally need a launderette across the road.

6. Where can you dry clothes? Remember that a small area that isn't well ventilated or heated will become damp and mould will form.

7. Is the kitchen big enough for all of your appliances and the number of people in the house? How much kitchen stuff will each of you have? What are the arrangements for rubbish collection and recycling?

8. Heating bills – I know some students will switch off the heating to save money for alternative entertainment, but you'll stay a lot warmer, be free of draughts and reduce the likelihood of damp if the property is double-glazed, insulated properly and the heating system is efficient. This includes water-based heating radiators being internally clean and bled of air. If the radiators are on, check if they are hotter at the top than the bottom. If there is a difference it's a sign they have air trapped in them and won't reach full temperature without being bled. It's also important to have independently controlled radiators so you can change the temperature in each room. If the heating isn't on, can you find another way to check it actually works?

9. Consider what the accommodation will be like at night and do rooms let enough light in during the day? (If not it will be a less cheery place and your lighting bills will be higher.)

10. Is the property detached, i.e. is there a space between your house and the ones next door on both sides? If you and your housemates are likely to be noisy then a detached house is great for keeping the neighbours from continually complaining, especially if they have families.

11. Conversely, can you hear your neighbours? This is another good reason for also visiting in the evening when your neighbours are at home.

12. Take a torch with you so you can check badly-lit areas. I suggest viewing the inside of the property first, as this is more important.

If you don't like the inside, it's pointless wasting time looking around the outside. Also, if it's wet outside, you will be more likely to drag soil and mud into the house. We will therefore cover the external points to look for after these internal ones.

13. Are the beds and furniture in a good condition? **The bed MUST be comfortable** – look at the condition of the mattress and lie down on it, as it's the most important piece of furniture you will have.

> **The mattress is THE most important item of furniture. Make sure it is comfortable, supportive and doesn't slump. Mattresses are best replaced after seven to 10 years, but frequently landlords buy cheap ones and fail to replace them after the recommended time limit. Poor sleep and backache can result from this, but it may not be immediately apparent.**

14. Is there a desk and chair for you to work at, and are there enough electrical sockets and a broadband connection within easy reach? USB sockets will be a bonus, as they will make charging your phone and computer much easier.

> **At this point it is also worth checking your mobile to make sure that you get an excellent signal and internet connection.**

15. Do you have a separate phone line so you aren't sharing a router? Are there phone sockets in each room or, if not, how can broadband be wired up and what speed is it? Is this included within the rental price? Make sure that the phone will be connected should you agree to move in. You don't want the expense of a reconnection, as it's usually around £80.

16. What type of flooring has been installed in your room and the communal areas? If it's carpets, check for stains. Also, remember that laminate is a lot easier to clean, but if the room above you has laminate flooring then you may hear people walking across it or

moving furniture. So check the room above and try to get someone in hard soles to walk across the room whilst you listen downstairs.

(I once lived in a new two-storey flat where we had an oak floor installed. We had complaints from the flat below because they could hear my girlfriend walking across the floor in her high-heeled shoes, so this didn't work well.)

17. Do all the kitchen appliances work correctly, e.g. the fridge, freezer, oven, hob, microwave? If there are more than five of you, are there two of each of these appliances, as you may need them? (You will certainly need a microwave as well as an oven.)

18. Check that the oven has been cleaned and the freezer defrosted - you don't want to be faced with either of these laborious tasks should you decide to move in.

19. Are there any signs of mould, damp or vermin (usually scratch marks or small dark flecks or droppings on floors and surfaces)? Check the kitchen cupboards. I recently helped a friend repair a leak. He was worried that it might have affected the flat below so we paid his neighbours a visit. Although there was no leak, thankfully, the tenants complained that the landlord hadn't sorted out their rodent problem. They showed us the kitchen cupboard – rats had eaten through the back of it to get at food that had been spilled and not cleaned up. The Thames, where the flats were near, is known for its rodent population, but seeing what they had done here was an education. Keep food wrapped up. If you hear scratching, don't ignore it. Inform the landlord. If there is a hole, get it blocked up!

20. Does the property smell? If so, what is the source of it? It may be damp, in which case you need to investigate further, or it could just be the current tenants and their cooking!

21. Are there curtains or blinds of a reasonable quality to provide privacy and keep the sun off your face early in the morning? Pull

the curtains across to make sure they meet in the middle. Drop down the blinds to check if they are likely to keep the room sufficiently dark, especially if the window is east facing and will catch the morning sunlight. Replacing curtains may be expensive and it's unlikely that the landlord will pay for them. However, if you make a note of what type of curtain hanging you have, you can check the prices on Google or at a large store such as Dunelm or Argos.

22. Look for stains or damp on the walls, ceilings, carpets and curtains (especially at the bottom and on the inside) and around all radiators and connecting plumbing pipes (copper pipes go green). Check for black spots on the silicone around the bath too. These will need explaining because you don't want a problem persisting or deteriorating, or for you to be blamed for it. If the stains are at floor level on the ground floor it could be a sign of a more substantial damp problem.

23. Check that the radiators are fitted with a numbered valve, and check that the valve can be turned. This is a temperature control and it's important for living comfortably. They are known as TRVs –Thermostatic Radiator Valves (*see figure 7 below*).

Figure 7 - Photo of TRV. Thermostatic Radiator Valve

24. For health reasons, you don't want to be living in a room with mould. Try to check walls, especially behind the bed and furniture in the bedrooms.

25. Open the windows and doors to make sure they fit properly and are not rotten or distorted. If they are double-glazed, have a look for any condensation inside the glazing – if there is any, it will need repairing or replacing (and it's not as expensive as most people think. It's quick to replace a sealed unit – the frame doesn't even need to be removed). This is something you should ask to be fixed before you move in.

26. Are the bedrooms well ventilated? Some double-glazed units are installed with only one small window that can be opened. This means it's likely to get incredibly hot in the summer.

27. Flush the toilet to make sure it works and that it doesn't drip or continue to run once the cistern has refilled. The noise will disturb your sleep and metered water will cost you more money.

28. What type of fuse board does the property have? A consumer unit/circuit breaker (*see figure 8*) is the safest (for you and your equipment), and if one of the breakers trips out (switches off) you only have to go to the unit and switch it back on again (assuming the fault was temporary). Old-fashioned fuse boards (*figure 9*) are less safe and fuses are a real pain to replace. If a fuse blows, you have to try and find out which one, frequently in the dark, which means guessing which fuse (they are seldom marked, e.g. lighting, sockets, cooker) so I recommend that you do NOT move in unless there has been an upgrade to circuit breakers.

My view is that properties should no longer have these fuse boards. If a property has one then the landlord may be skimping on other areas.

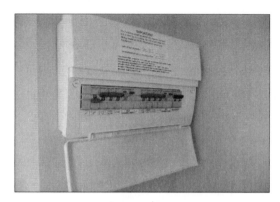

Figure 8 - Photo of consumer unit RCB

Figure 9 - Photo of old-style fuse board

Of course, you can always ask for it to be replaced prior to you moving in, but it will cost the landlord approximately £300 to have one fitted, so don't expect them to do it. However, if they are faced with void periods then they may well agree to invest in one. No harm in asking.

29. Ask if the loft can be used for storage and if so, try to have a look to make sure how much space there is and whether it is easily accessible. There should be a light switch (if not, ask for one to be

installed). Be careful about going into the loft because if it isn't properly boarded you could fall through the ceiling between the rafters. I have to admit that I once lost my footing and put a foot through a ceiling, but it could have been much worse! The loft should have thick insulation and if it is also boarded this will not only provide useful storage space but reduce heat loss and help you save on your energy bills too.

30. Is there a notice board? (It will be much better if there is, but if there isn't, can one be put up?)

31. Is there an ironing board? There should be – you don't want to have to pay for one.

32. Are there wastepaper baskets in the rooms? Has the landlord supplied buckets, mops, a dustpan and brush and a clothes airer? Ok, they aren't expensive but buying them is an inconvenience and if they are provided it's a good indication the landlord cares and understands your lifestyle.

Safety and Security

✓ Are there enough working fire alarms (at least one on each floor)? Are these battery operated or electrically linked?

✓ Are any of the plug sockets cracked or damaged? If so, they must be repaired. However, bear in mind that a decent landlord wouldn't allow them to be in this state, so it's an indication that other corners are being cut.

✓ Are there enough sockets in each room for a TV, computer, printer, hairdryer, charger, table lamps, music devices and broadband? You don't want to overload electrical points or have a batch of extension leads (which can overload a socket and ultimately cause a fire).

✓ Is the furniture fire resistant? (Ideally, all pieces of furniture should still have labels attached, although this is only a legal requirement when they are being sold in a shop.)

✓ Has a fire blanket or fire extinguisher been provided? This isn't a legal requirement as fire departments usually say that they don't want tenants in HMOs fighting fires because they want them to get out quickly. However, some councils say they are mandatory!

✓ Do the entrance doors have decent, five-lever mortice deadlocks, and are there locks on all the bedroom doors? (Some landlords don't have them for fear of being made responsible for council tax on every room.) Are there locks on all the windows on the ground floor or basement? (These are important for security and may also help you reduce the cost of your insurance.) I believe that this is an essential requirement. On uPVC frames, the lock is normally integrated within the window handle.

✓ Are there full sets of keys for all of you? (This is essential.)

✓ Does the area feel safe at night?

For security reasons, I recommend that before committing to a property you take a trip back at night. This will also help you ensure there aren't any additional disturbances (e.g. a rough pub or nightclub over the road).

✓ Are there any wooden window frames that are rotten or have gaps between the frame and the wall? (These will be draughty as well as insecure.)

✓ An alarm box on the outside of the house is preferable as a visible deterrent, even if it's not wired up. On the inside, it's obviously preferable if there is an infrared motion detector, for when you are all out of the property. The keypad for this is usually located in the hall, but you will need to ensure that it's activated and is free to use (some are activated by payment of a large monthly fee).

✓ If there is side access to the rear of the house, is it secure and is there a gate with a lock?

✓ If there is a ladder outside, make sure it can be locked away. If not, it's a major security risk, so request that either a lockable bracket is installed or it is removed (what chance is there that you will use it?).

 Make a note of **all issues** so you can inform the agent/landlord about them and ensure it's in the contract that they will be fixed **BEFORE** you move in.

External Features

Figure 10 - High-maintenance garden. This is likely to be your responsibility.

✓ Try to have a look at the roof as best you can from the ground level. Broken or missing tiles may mean a leak, which may not yet be showing in the ceilings or walls.

✓ Check the walls for any damp or discoloured patches. These are usually caused by broken gutters or a toilet cistern overflow.

✓ Is there a garage and can it be used for storage? If you've got a bike, remember to think about where you are going to put it.

✓ Is an external bin provided and how big is it? You will need more than one standard-sized wheelie bin and another for recyclables, especially if collections are only every two weeks. These should be provided by your landlord and can be bought from the council. Your landlord should have them on the inventory.

✓ How big is the garden? (*See figure 10.*) How is it maintained and by whom? Lots of bushes and plants look nice but they take a lot of time and effort to look after. Make sure that such maintenance is the landlord's responsibility. If it doesn't specify in the tenancy agreement that it is your responsibility, then it will be the landlord's.

There is a lot of information in this chapter and all of it is really important, so do make sure you download the checklists and make lots of notes. You don't want to find yourself agreeing to renting accomodation for a certain period, only to find it blighted by issues and safety hazards. Do your 'due diligence'!

CHAPTER FIVE

Type of Let/Tenancy & Things Landlords Cannot Do

Figure 11 - These are the rules!

Nearly everyone who has been to uni knows of someone who has been evicted, i.e. told to leave. Sometimes you hear of instances where the student was told to pack his bags within a week.

What about the landlord turning up and demanding to be let in without warning?

Well, this chapter will help you put a stop to illegal and unfair practices.

Type of Let/Tenancy

Landlords have a number of options on how they can manage the renting out of a property, so you need to know what these are and who is *responsible for handling any issues that arise*. This way, you can defend yourself with confidence.

Basically, the landlord is the client of the letting agent, so, theoretically at least, all fees should be paid by the landlord. However, in the muddied waters of property rentals, the commercial reality is not so clear-cut. Tenants are usually charged for a number of services. Some of these are reasonable, but many are not and some are duplications of what the agent charges the landlord. Effectively, they are a profit-boosting opportunity, as many students are seen as naïve and unlikely to question what they are paying for.

In Chapter 9 I will highlight the likely fee charges, but for the moment the following is a broad outline of the different types of lets that landlords are most likely to be using.

Self-managing landlords

This is where the landlord is in **complete control of the tenancy**. They probably advertise privately for tenants and are not using a rental agency (although some may choose to do that as well).

As you will be dealing with the landlord directly, it *should* make it easier to get repairs done in the house, but the reality is frequently the opposite.

It's important to ensure that the landlord doesn't cut corners in their rental agreement when it comes to the handling of your deposit and other legal requirements. Again, we will cover these in more detail so that you can be prepared.

Letting only/finders fee

This is where a **landlord pays an agent to advertise the property, find tenants and complete reference checks and paperwork.** In addition to the fee they charge the landlord, the agent may also try to charge the tenants a reference and administration fee. It's a bit like Ryanair really: everything is extra, so make sure they don't charge you if you use their office loo! As previously referred to, these fees may be made illegal.

In this type of letting, the deposit and initial rental payment will be taken by the agent, with all subsequent payments being made direct to the landlord, probably by setting up a direct debit or standing order payment (see 'Payment Methods' in Chapter 9, for more detailed explanations).

 It is very important for you to ensure that the agreements you had with the letting agent are included in the contract with the landlord. This is because the landlord may be unaware of the nice chat you had with the agent where he promised certain things. Additionally, as with any financial transaction, you need a receipt.

Letting and rent collection

As above, but with the **additional responsibility of collecting the rent on the landlord's behalf.** The landlord is still responsible for repairs and maintenance.

Full management

The letting agent is responsible for everything and organises repairs and maintenance. In this situation, you may never speak to or meet your landlord.

A downside to this arrangement is that the agents can be slow to resolve issues as they may have a restricted budget for repairs and will therefore need to contact the landlord for approval for expenditure above a specific level. This can consume your time but you must persist in chasing them in order to get things put right.

However, the good news is that unlike many landlords, the agent should have a list of reliable tradesmen who they can call in an emergency.

Types of Tenancy

There are a couple of different types of tenancy agreement, as defined in law. However, the one that you will invariably be required to sign is an **Assured Shorthold Tenancy (AST)**. I have been informed that, surprisingly, many landlords don't even have such a document. Frankly, this is madness on their part. If a landlord doesn't have an AST contract, I reckon they are naive at best. An AST is an agreement regarding what each party is responsible for, so why wouldn't they have one? I'd be suspicious that they were trying to avoid their agreed responsibilities and would therefore be at risk of pulling flankers on recharges and other agreed terms. It's inexcusable not to have an AST, as they can be downloaded from the internet for a low fee, or via a letting agent. These days you don't have to pay a solicitor several hundred pounds to get one drafted.

> **If your prospective landlord doesn't offer an AST then I would either find another property or insist that one is drafted at their expense, so you have security of tenure until the end of the academic year.**

Legally you have security of tenure with or without a contract so long as you can prove that rent has been paid, but such a dispute will be too much hassle and stress and take up a lot of your time.

Tenancy or licence

In landlord and tenant law, there is a difference between a Licence and a Tenancy. This is important as many agreements are incorrectly titled as licences. In a licence, the owner of the property gives someone permission to share the property but does not give them an interest in the property (this means that the property is shared with the landlord, as it is also their home, or that a person employed by the landlord lives in the property and manages it).

A tenancy gives the tenant a legal interest in the property and the exclusive right to occupy it. Effectively, the landlord is loaning the property to the tenant(s) for a period of time in exchange for rent and the right for the landlord to get the property back when the tenancy has ended (legally known as the 'reversion'). In reality, it's more complicated than this. Nevertheless, the landlord in the AST does lose many of his or her rights over the property in exchange for the right to receive rent.

ASTs are good news for you as a tenant! They mean the landlord should only enter the property with your permission.

The landlord **must give a minimum of 24-hours' written notice and visit during normal daylight hours,** unless the tenant asks to change this. The landlord may not simply demand to enter, but if he has to carry out a legal obligation, such as checking fire safety equipment or having a gas safety inspection, you must not prevent him from doing this at a time convenient to you. This includes doing viewings with prospective new tenants and applies equally to letting agents.

ASTs are not a charter for tenants to think they can do what they like with impunity. If the tenant is obstructive then the landlord can gain access, but only if they follow certain procedures.

A very important aspect is that a tenant has *'security of tenure,'* which means that he can only be evicted from the property *if* the landlord follows certain legal procedures.

The tenancy agreement would normally state that the tenancy is for a specific period of time (e.g. nine months). This is known as a *fixed term tenancy.*

Once the fixed term comes to an end, it doesn't mean the tenant has to leave.

The law implies that the tenancy continues on the same terms as the fixed term tenancy, but on the basis of an additional, unspecified period – hence the term Statutory Periodic Tenancy, which is also known as the 'Rollover Period'. If your rent is paid monthly then it will be a monthly periodic tenancy, if it's weekly then a weekly periodic tenancy, and so on.

Periodic tenancies can continue indefinitely until the landlord or tenant does something to end the tenancy in a 'recognised' way.

In order to terminate a tenancy, the landlord or tenant needs to give formal notice as per the AST, or, in extreme cases, the landlord can go through the court to get an Order for Possession.

In the 'Rollover Period', the tenant can give one tenancy period (usually one month) notice at any time. The landlord must follow a legal process covered by either Section 8 or Section 21 of the Housing Act 1988, unless the tenant decides to vacate the property (e.g. handing back the keys).

Many landlords believe they can take possession of the property after the fixed term of the agreement and that a tenant remaining in the property is a squatter. To clarify:

Landlords cannot take possession of the property simply because the fixed term has ended.

You may be offered a licence, which in fact is an AST. A licence has a number of additional responsibilities, e.g. the provision of meals, but the key issue is that if your contract grants exclusive possession then effectively this will be deemed to be an AST even if it is labelled a licence.

Resident landlords

Where the owner of the property lives in the same building, a letting is generally excluded from the definition of an AST. The 'Resident Landlord' must be occupying it as their main home at the time the tenancy is granted.

There are two types of Resident Landlord situations, which are:

1. **Sharing accommodation with the licencee** (the tenant is then a *lodger*).

2. **The tenant occupies self-contained accommodation in the same building** (other than a purpose-built block of flats, where the tenancy is regulated under 'common law' and not the Housing Act 1988). Self-contained accommodation in the same building relates to another type of tenancy and is governed by different tenancy laws known as '**Assured Tenancies**'.

There are legal advantages for a landlord if the tenancy is a licence rather than an AST, which is why some of them (incorrectly) name their agreement a licence. The phrase, "If it looks like a duck, swims like a duck and quacks like a duck then it probably is a duck" comes to mind! These landlords are trying it on so that there will be less hassle if they want to remove a tenant. So, if it looks like a duck...in law their 'licence' will be treated as an AST and they will have to follow the lengthy procedure to remove a tenant.

If a landlord gives you a licence agreement and tries to make you leave without due legal process, the **law will protect you if you are deemed**

to be a tenant rather than a lodger. In a recent legal case, the judge upheld the fact that the students renting were tenants not lodgers. This was because despite having a main residence elsewhere in the UK, they were living in the property during term time, which constituted most of the year.

It's unlikely that you will be signing an agreement that is something other than an AST, so throughout this book I will be assuming that the tenancy you have is one of these.

Sublet

This is where a **tenant rents out their property to a different tenant.** I know of entrepreneurial students who have done this in order to make a profit on the "arbitragem," i.e. the difference in what they receive from their tenant to what they have to pay to their landlord.

However, there is more than likely a clause in the tenancy agreement that prohibits this, and it will undoubtedly invalidate the insurance on the property as well as create serious complications over such issues as tenancy agreements, repairs, damages and inventories.

If you are considering doing this as a way to create some income (it's a strategy done on a bigger scale by some investors and is called Rent to Rent, R2R, Let to Rent, Rent to Let or variations on this theme), I suggest you initially get the landlord's written permission and then take legal advice. It is a complicated, time-consuming and risky business.

This is why you must remember…

> **…before you hand over any cash, you need to know that the 'landlord' is the *real owner* of the property.**

This is because it has been known for people who sublet to run off with people's deposits and rental payments.

Property Ownership

It's important to know that your landlord *actually owns the property,* as there are a couple of issues related to this.

A couple of years ago, a friend of mine, who is a London landlord, left one of his homes empty for less than a week. When the agents reported a break-in, it transpired a bogus landlord and agent were responsible. They had advertised the property online and taken deposits from tenants using fake contracts. They obviously ran off with the cash and presumably the mobile phone they used was a pay-as-you-go.

To counter this, make sure you visit agents in their offices and don't hand over money to a landlord without seeing their proof of identity (get a copy of their driving licence or passport). Write down their address too.

If the person purporting to be the landlord is NOT the owner according to the Land Registry, then you need to urgently make enquiries to establish who IS the landlord and get their contact details. Then establish what the connection is with the person you believed to be the landlord. This isn't a situation that is rife across the country, but there have been an increasing number of cases of absent owners having their properties taken over and rented out by opportunists or villains.

The property world also uses the phrase 'creative deals' to describe techniques being taught to aspiring property investors around the country. These involve such obtuse terms as Lease Options, Rent-to-Rent, Let-to-Rent, Rent-to-Let, Delayed Completions and Instalment Contracts.

Examples of these are where a landlord/owner has got tired of the everyday hassles of being a landlord. In order to pay his mortgage without doing the work, he has therefore rented out the property to another investor who then acts as a landlord (effectively they are managing the property) and does the marketing and rent collection in order to make a margin/arbitrage on the difference in price between what the investor pays the owner and what he receives from the tenants. In principle this is good, creative deal making, but it means that the property is being sub-let, and this may be in breach of the landlord's mortgage terms.

If a property that you are renting is one of these sub-lets and mortgaged, then you could be at risk of sudden eviction should your landlord default on their payments or contravene any of the lender's terms.

The issue here is that if there is a mortgage on the property and the owner fails to pay it, then where does the contract between the intermediary landlord/investor and the tenants stand, especially if the mortgage company needs to repossess the property?

Ask your agent how long they have been renting out this property and what proof they have of its ownership.

If they haven't rented the property previously then ask them to confirm ownership via the Land Registry.

Ultimately, you can check it yourself at www.landregistry.gov.uk/ There is a small fee to pay but at the moment this is only £3.

The National Landlords Association (NLA) has issued a warning about the number of rental scams on a well-known item-listing website. Apparently, unsuspecting potential tenants, usually from overseas, reply to advertisements on the website for rental accommodation in the UK. After exchanging emails, tenants are asked to send money to the 'landlord'.

Having sent the money, when the tenants attempt to make contact with the 'landlord' or collect keys to the property, they discover he or she is not contactable and the potential tenants have been defrauded. A clue is that the letters from the fake landlords are often written in poor English.

In the latest scam, the 'landlord' claims to be a member of the NLA and uses the NLA logo and fake stationery. They also copy the bona fide

NLA Tenant Check service or use fake letters from NLA local representatives to support their demands.

As a result of this, the NLA recommends that overseas applicants who need to secure accommodation before they arrive in the UK should first seek the help of the employer or university they are coming to.

Tenants wishing to check whether a prospective landlord is a member of the NLA should ask them for their membership number, then go to: www.landlords.org.uk/member-verification.

CHAPTER SIX
Landlord Responsibilities & Compliance

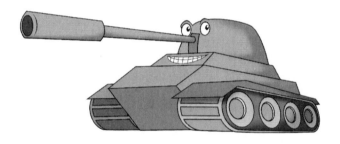

Figure 12 - Legislation is there to protect you!

Presumably you have a virus checker on your computer and you are able to block malware and identify phishing emails? It amazes me how effective even free virus checkers are these days. A dozen years ago I had three hard drives that were trashed in quick succession as a result of attacks on Microsoft.

Legislation is like a virus checker. It's designed to block malware. However, it has to be installed correctly and needs constant updates, as the rogues find ways to beat the protection.

Installing and maintaining this virus checker needs ongoing management. In the case of legislation relating to property, councils don't appear to have the time or inclination to manage it. This means that tenants have unreliable protection so they are likely to experience 'phishing' and malware attacks on their finances, even from uninformed landlords (and there are LOTS of them).

Continuing the metaphor, I'll do with you what I did with my daughter years ago. We used to play a computer game called Doom. It was a fun beat 'em up game and we got frustrated by continually having to go back to the beginning, having been vaporised scores of times. We did some research on the internet and found cheat sheets, so when our character was losing energy or ammunition, instead of getting blasted and having to start again, we used the shortcuts to replenish ammunition, get more armour and get instant first aid.

So, treat this as your own cheat sheet to find where the extra ammo, armour and first aid are located.

There are many legal references in this chapter. Don't let this deter you from reading it because most of these rules *benefit you*.

You don't need to know *all* the details, just understand the principles and use them as a reference in case you need to get the landlord to provide the facilities or services that you are entitled to.

In case any reader gets excited by legislation or loves to unravel government legal speak, I've added the regulation numbers as a cross-reference so you can read more.

In the Private Rented Sector, the accommodation that you will be renting will be one of the following:

→ **A room in a private house**

This is where you rent a room in a house where the landlord currently lives. Many international students arrange to live with families, so this may be more appropriate for them.

→ **Private flat**

Even if there are just two of you sharing, this will be way outside the budgets of most students.

→ **A house or flat share**

Where you rent with a number of friends or other students. These are the most common arrangements, and by their definition most of them will be **Houses of Multiple Occupation.**

The legal definition of an HMO is set out in Section 254 onwards in the Housing Act 2004. If you *really feel inclined to check it out*, refer to www.legislation.gov.uk website.

A 'house share', where a property is rented out by at least three people who are not from one 'household' (e.g. a family) but share facilities like the bathroom and kitchen, is also known as an HMO.

Of greater importance is a 'large' HMO. **It is mandatory for every 'large' HMO property to be *registered with the local council.***

Councils can interpret the definitions slightly differently, however, a large HMO is broadly defined as:

a) Rented to *five or more people* who form more than one household (blood-related family or cohabiting couples, although a landlord and his household living with two tenants is excluded from licensing).

b) In *three or more* storeys.

c) Having *shared amenities* such as a bathroom, toilet or kitchen facilities.

There are understandably more safety issues with a 'large HMO', so it's important that your landlord *complies with the licensing laws.*

Once the council has inspected and approved the property they will issue a certificate to the landlord.

House in Multiple Occupation (HMO) Rules

Now, getting a bit more specific on areas of the HMO regulations that are important to you, there are **Management Regulations** that detail the responsibilities of landlords and tenants. Yes, you have some responsibilities as well. The following are the key points from *The Management of Houses in Multiple Occupation (England) Regulations 2006.* (Note that it doesn't cover all the points within the regulations, although I have provided a cross-reference to the relevant regulation). *There are also slightly different regulations for Wales and more differences in Scotland, as they have a separate legal system.*

The reference to a 'Manager' is how it's set out in the regulations, as it could apply to a landlord or his agent.

→ **Duty of the Manager to provide information** *(Regulation 3)*

The manager must ensure that:

✓ His name, address and telephone number are made available to each household and displayed in a prominent position within the property.

→ **Duty of the Manager to take Safety Measures** *(Regulation 4)*

The manager must ensure that:

✓ All means of escape from fire (including any fire-fighting equipment and fire alarms) are free from obstruction and are maintained and in good order and repair.

✓ Notices indicating the location of means of escape within the HMO are displayed and clearly visible to the occupants (this does not apply where there are four or fewer occupiers).

✓ All reasonable measures are taken to protect the occupiers of the HMO from injury, having regard to the design, structural condition and number of occupiers in the HMO.

✓ Any roof or balcony is made safe and that access is prevented as long as they remain unsafe.

✓ Any window or sill which is at or near floor level has bars or safeguards as necessary to protect the occupiers against the danger of accidents which may be caused in connection with those windows.

→ **Water Supply and Drainage** *(Regulation 5)*

The manager must ensure that:

✓ The water supply and drainage system are kept in good, clean working condition. In particular, cisterns and tanks that are used for the storage of water for drinking or other domestic purposes are covered to keep the water clean, and fittings which are liable to damage by frost are protected from this damage.

✓ The manager must not do anything to interfere with the supply of water or drainage.

→ **Gas and Electricity** *(Regulation 6)*

The manager must ensure that:

✓ Every gas appliance is inspected and tested on an annual basis by a Gas Safe Registered engineer, and that a copy of the latest gas certificate is supplied to the local authority within seven days of receiving a written request.

✓ Every electrical installation is inspected and tested at least every five years by a qualified electrician and a certificate obtained. This must also be supplied to the local authority within seven days of receiving a written request. The manager must not do anything to interfere with the supply of gas or electricity.

→ **Common Parts, Fixtures, Fittings, Appliances and Outside** *(Regulation 7)*

The manager must ensure that:

✓ The common parts (including windows and other means of ventilation) are maintained in good, clean repair, free from obstruction, and that handrails and banisters are replaced or provided where necessary.

✓ Any stair coverings are safely fixed and kept in good repair.

✓ The common parts should be fitted with adequate light fittings that are available at all times by every occupier.

✓ Fixtures, fittings or appliances used by two or more households should be maintained in good and safe repair and in a clean working order. However, this doesn't apply to any fixtures, fittings or appliances that the occupier is entitled to move from the HMO.

✓ Any outbuildings, yards, areas and forecourts in common use are kept in repair, clean and in good order, and that any garden belonging to the HMO is kept in a safe and tidy condition; that boundary walls, fences and railings (including any basement area railings) are maintained in a good and safe state of repair so they are not a danger to the occupiers.

✓ Note that 'common parts' for which the manager has responsibility include entrance doors (including to occupiers' own rooms), stairs, passages and corridors, lobbies, entrances, balconies, porches and steps – basically the parts of the property used by the occupiers to gain access to their own accommodation or any other part of the property shared by the occupiers.

✓ If any part of the HMO is not in use the manager shall ensure that any area directly giving access to it is kept clean and free from refuse and litter.

→ **Living Accommodation** *(Regulation 8)*

The manager must ensure that:

✓ Each unit of living accommodation and any furniture supplied with it are in clean condition at the beginning of the person's occupation of it.

✓ That the internal structures, any fixtures, fittings or appliances, windows or any other means of ventilation, are maintained in good repair and in clean working order. However, this doesn't apply to any fixtures, fittings or appliances that the occupier is entitled to move from the HMO, nor to damage caused by the occupier failing to comply with the terms of his tenancy agreement or if he fails to conduct himself in a reasonable manner.

→ **House Refuse** *(Regulation 9)*

The manager must ensure that:

✓ Sufficient and suitable litter bins are provided and are adequate for the requirements of each household for the storage of refuse pending collection; and to make arrangements for the disposal of rubbish with regard to the local authority's collection service.

→ **Duties of Occupiers** *(Regulation 10)*

Every occupier of the HMO must:

✓ Conduct himself in a way that will not hinder or frustrate the manager in the performance of his duties.

✓ Allow the manager at all reasonable times to enter rooms for any purposes connected with the carrying out of any duty imposed on him by these Regulations.

✓ Give the manager any information he may reasonably require for the purpose of carrying out his duties.

✓ Take reasonable care not to damage anything which the manager is obliged to supply, maintain or repair under these regulations.

✓ Comply with arrangements made by the manager for the storage and disposal of litter.

✓ Comply with the reasonable instructions of the manager in respect of any means of escape from fire, the prevention of fire and the use of fire equipment.

→ **General** *(Regulation 11)*

✓ Any duty imposed by these Regulations to maintain or keep in repair are to be taken as requiring a standard of maintenance or repair that is reasonable, taking account of the age, character and prospective life of the property and the locality in which it is situated. (In other words, the standards required in an address in Mayfair are different to those in a scruffy bedsit above a chippy in an unsafe, rundown area.)

✓ In addition, local councils also introduce their own 'Locally Adopted Standards' that landlords have to comply with. It is worth acquiring a copy of these so you can understand the minimum standards that are acceptable.

If you are living in an HMO and your landlord is not complying with any of this, then you might want to *politely refer them to the Regulations* – not just to be a stickler for the rules, but also to ensure that the conditions of the property are of the right standard for you. It is a powerful negotiating tool.

Excessive cold is an unacceptable 'hazard'. Each room should have a heating appliance that can maintain the room temperature at a minimum of 18c in bedrooms and 21c in living rooms, when the outside temperature is -1c, and should be available at all times.

Don't accept anything less!

You should also be aware that from 1st April 2018 there will be additional legislation so that tenants can force a landlord to bring the property up to a minimum EPC rating of E. This should result in properties being better insulated and therefore warmer.

HMO licensing and fire safety

For safety reasons, it's imperative that all HMOs comply with these. **If your property doesn't comply, your lives are at risk**, so you either need to rent an alternative property or ensure that the property will comply before you move in.

> **It is a legal requirement for an HMO to have a Fire Risk Assessment carried out and retained on file, so ask the agent or landlord for a copy before you sign an agreement.**

A summary of fire rules that apply to an HMO:

1. The provision of an integrated (i.e. mains-powered, not battery-powered) smoke alarm system will be required for HMOs with more than two storeys. The alarms must also be interlinked.

2. Fire warning systems such as fire alarms and heat or smoke detectors should be placed throughout the building, particularly in escape routes and high-risk areas, such as kitchens.

3. Fire warning systems should be serviced and checked regularly.

4. Fire equipment such as fire extinguishers and fire blankets: At least one fire extinguisher of the correct type should be provided on every floor and checked regularly. At least one fire blanket should be provided in each shared kitchen. (However, there is a contradiction here because fire departments want people out of a property rather than risking their lives trying to put out a fire, so they don't always want fire extinguishers, which can be difficult to use, to be provided).

5. An escape route that can resist fire, smoke and fumes long enough for everyone to leave. This could be an external fire escape, or

specially treated fire-resistant internal stairs and corridors. All doors leading to the escape route must also be fire resistant and must close automatically.

6. As a result of The Smoke and Carbon Monoxide Alarm (England) Regulations 2015, smoke alarms are to be installed on every storey and a carbon monoxide alarm in any room containing a solid fuel burning appliance.

For current regulations on fire saftey for HMOs in your area, visit www.gov.uk and type 'Fire Safety' in the search bar.

Regulations for all Rented Accommodation

The 2004 Housing Act requires the landlord to do several things about fire safety:

1. There has to be an *adequate means of escape.*

2. Depending on the size of the property, there may *have to be smoke alarms and fire extinguishing equipment.*

3. If the property is a House in Multiple Occupation (HMO), which is subject to licensing by your council, your landlord *must also comply with licence conditions in relation to fire safety.*

Smoke alarms

Under the 1999 Smoke Alarm Act, *all newly built houses (newer than 1992) must be fitted with a smoke alarm,* the minimum requirement being one alarm per floor.

The tenancy agreement should outline *who* is responsible for the maintenance of these alarms – it could be the letting agent, the landlord or you, the tenants. You must be sure of this before you sign.

Detectors should be sited 30 centimetres from walls and light fittings. This is because light fittings attract dust, which can cause false alarms and in the early stages of a fire, smoke doesn't always go right into the corner of the ceiling.

The landlord must provide his/her telephone number in 'common places' throughout the accommodation.

Furniture

The Furniture and Furnishings (Fire) (Safety) Regulations 1988 require the following:

✓ All new furniture (except mattresses, bed-bases, pillows, scatter cushions, seat pads, loose and stretch covers for furniture) must carry a display label at the point of sale. This is a retailer's responsibility, so the furniture in the accommodation should also comply with the regulations. If labels are missing, though, it doesn't mean that the items are not compliant.

The Regulations apply to any of the following that contain upholstery:

✓ Furniture (including nursery furniture and garden furniture that can be used indoors)

✓ Beds, headboards of beds, mattresses

✓ Sofa beds, futons and other convertibles

✓ Scatter cushions and seat pads

✓ Pillows

✓ Loose and stretch covers for furniture

The Regulations do not apply to:

✗ Furniture made before 1950 or reupholstery of furniture made before that date.

All furniture (new and second-hand) must meet the Fire Resistance Requirements:

✓ Furniture must pass a cigarette-resistance test.

✓ Cover fabric, whether for use in permanent or loose covers, must pass a match-resistance test.

✓ Filling materials for all furniture must pass ignitability tests.

Even if your accommodation is in a non-HMO regulated property, and even if there is no smoking permitted, ensure that a smoke detector is installed.

Non-HMOs must **also have a smoke alarm fitted on each floor**, although these can be battery operated and do not need to be linked together. If there aren't any, insist that your landlord fits them (they cost less than £10 for a battery-operated one, so there is no excuse). Also ensure that they are not positioned right in the corner of walls/ceilings, as smoke can take much longer to reach into the angles.

Electrical safety

Whilst (other than for HMOs) there is no statutory requirement to have safety checks on electrical installations, the Landlord and Tenant Act 1985 requires the landlord to ensure the electrical installation is safe when the tenancy begins and that it is maintained in a safe condition throughout that tenancy.

Inspections of the fixed installation by a competent person (generally a qualified electrician) to ensure safety and that the electrical system complies with current electrical regulations is required under management regulations for HMOs (whether licensable or not), at intervals of no more than five years.

The landlord's obligation is to ensure that the electrics are visually inspected at the turn of every tenancy or annually, whichever comes first.

A landlord must ensure that any portable electrical appliance supplied is 'safe', with no unacceptable risk of injury or death, or damage to property. They must undergo 'Portable Appliance Testing.'

Portable appliances are those that would normally have a plug fitted and include all mains voltage equipment such as kettles, toasters, washing machines and fridges. A 'competent person' should carry out this testing. It does not need to be a qualified electrician, but someone who has, for instance, been on a relevant training course and has suitable experience. The commonly heard term, PAT stands for Portable Appliance Testing for which there are approved training courses.

If you are aware of any faulty sockets or trip-switches/fuses blowing regularly, you should contact your landlord and confirm it in writing, so he can inspect and fix the problem.

Although there are no rules specifying response times, with any safety issue the landlord should respond *immediately*.

Electrical safety dos and don'ts

→ Don't overload your extension leads and adaptors with too many plugs. This is a fire risk.

→ If you are using an electrical heater, don't plug this into an adaptor or socket with other plugs. Heaters use a lot of electricity so should be plugged into a separate wall socket.

→ Don't twist, tightly bend or crush electrical leads or wires because they may split within their outer cable, which you won't be able to see, and this could cause a short-circuit potentially leading to a fire. On the same principle, don't run cables underneath carpets or rugs.

→ Unplug heaters and irons when they are not in use, rather than just switching off the appliance, as they generate a lot of heat and, needless to say, they can be very dangerous.

→ Don't drape washing over electrical heaters, especially convection heaters, as they need to have their vents open to release heat and blocking them can cause combustion.

Gas

As there are inherent risks involved when gas is supplied to a property, you need the reassurance that no shortcuts are being taken with your safety. In view of the risks, there are regulations that your landlord must adhere to.

Where there is gas supplied, at the start of any tenancy, the tenant must be given a copy of the Gas Safety Inspection Certificate.

Gas Safety Regulations make it mandatory that gas appliances must be maintained in a safe condition at all times. A breach of the Regulations is a criminal offence, enforced by the Health and Safety Executive (HSE). Gas Safety (Installation and Use) Regulations 1998.

Note that a landlord or agent may not contract out of their obligations under the Regulations by inserting a clause in the tenancy agreement that passes their responsibilities onto a tenant.

If there is such a clause then you can delete it before you sign it. Also, remember that it is important that all tenants are made aware of the location of the emergency shut-off valve to their accommodation and how it is operated.

All gas installers must be registered to work on gas appliances. Capita Group plc is now responsible for the registration of gas installers under the name Gas Safe. (Previously known as CORGI - and some may still refer to that name.)

Registered installers have been trained in gas safety and the standards needed for appliances and installations. Due to the dangers of faulty appliances, it is illegal to use a gas installer who is not registered.

All Gas Safe registered installers must carry a Gas Safe ID card, so you should always ask to see it before any installer begins work on your gas appliances.

The landlord must have the property checked for safety within 12 months of gas being installed and then at least every 12 months by a Gas Safe registered installer.

The landlord's responsibilities are to:

→ Ensure a gas safety check has been carried out on each appliance and flue within the 12-month period before any tenancy commences and take remedial action or disconnect any appliance that fails a safety check.

→ Give a copy of the safety check record or certificate to any new tenant before they move in or to an existing tenant(s) within 28 days.

→ Keep a record of the safety check made on each appliance for two years.

→ Ensure that gas appliances, fittings and flues are maintained in a safe condition.

Make sure that you get a copy of a current Gas Safe certificate before you move in and if the certificate expires before the end of your tenancy, make a note in your diary two weeks prior to this date to prompt your agent/landlord to get a new one.

Tenants also have responsibilities imposed upon them by the Gas Safety Regulations and landlords should inform tenants of this in the tenancy agreement. This would include:

→ Reporting any defect.

→ Not using an appliance that is known or thought to be unsafe.

As from 1st October 2015, a CO (carbon monoxide) alarm has to be installed in any room containing a solid fuel burning appliance (e.g. a coal fire, wood burning stove).

Apparently, the symptoms of CO poisoning are a bit like flu, so it's easy to misdiagnose it. The symptoms include a slight headache that progressively gets worse, nausea, dizziness and drowsiness, so just be aware that such an illness, especially if it recurs or refuses to go away, may be more serious than flu.

The good news about living with CO alarms is that they are not like smoke alarms. They are not set off by making toast or frying bacon. If a CO monitor goes off it means there is a problem, so you need to take immediate action. It is recommended that you open all windows, get out of the accommodation and immediately call your landlord or letting agent.

When you are negotiating to rent accommodation, request that your landlord fit a Carbon Monoxide (CO) alarm. (If applicable, i.e. there is a solid fuel burning appliance.)

Also be aware that since 31st October 1998, any room converted to use as sleeping accommodation should not contain the following types of gas appliances:

× A gas fire

× A gas space heater

× A gas water heater (including a gas boiler) of 14 kilowatts gross input or less, or any instantaneous water heater unless it is room sealed or has an atmosphere-sensing device.

Don't rent a property with any of the above in the bedroom.

There is a viewing checklist in the downloads section of **www.smartstudentguides.com/bookdocs**

CHAPTER SEVEN

Action After the Viewing

Pre-Signing

Assuming that you are now happy about the property and you want to rent it, you obviously need to visit the agents to complete the paperwork.

Set up a convenient time with them rather than just turning up at their office, as it may take an hour to complete the documentation. Also, as there will be items to negotiate over, you'll need to do some preparation.

Before visiting the agents

You and your housemates will all need to be organised, as this is a negotiation rather than a simple administrative exercise. If you are looking to 'chip' (reduce) the rent, then make sure you all know how you intend to approach this. It's probably sensible to agree on a spokesperson/lead negotiator, as this will help prevent the temptation for someone else to jump in and agree to something too early.

When signing

Try to attend at the same time.

Prior to signing your tenancy agreement, your agent or landlord should request that you provide the following from each tenant/sharer, so that they can comply with the *"Right to Rent"* legislation. The aim of this is to identify illegal immigrants, but everyone has to be checked. In my opinion this is tedious bureaucracy, as rogues will avoid the laws anyway, but I'll spare you a rant.

So, you will need:

✓ A recent bank statement showing your current address.

✓ Bank details for your payments, including: account name, bank name, six-digit sort code and bank account number.

✓ Photo identification (passport and preferably a driving licence as well – original not a copy).

✓ Guarantor details.

 As a result of the Retaliatory Eviction and the Deregulation Act 2015, for **all new tenancies,** the following should be handed to you *before the start of a tenancy,* otherwise the landlord cannot serve a Section 21 (eviction) notice!

→ **An Energy Performance Certificate (EPC)** must be shown at the property viewing because it's deemed to be part of the decision-making process. In my opinion this is a costly, bureaucratic exercise that has little use because you can see for yourself the most important issues, i.e. double-glazing, insulation and heating controls, and you will know whether you want to go to the expense of buying different light bulbs. However, landlords still have to provide the reports. (You may want to bear in mind that from April 2018, a property will not be allowed for letting unless the EPC rating is above category E. However, this is a low standard and if it is in this category you should have already walked away from the property.)

→ **A copy of the Department for Communities and Local Government's document,** *'How to rent: the checklist for renting in England.*

→ A valid annual **Gas Safety Certificate.**

→ **Deposit protection** documents.

→ **HMO licence.** (Where necessary.)

This is champion information to negotiate with once you have moved in, as landlords who *fail to provide these* cannot issue a Section 21 Notice of Possession. (They can use a different notice if you don't pay your rent). The legislation itself protects you from eviction anyway, even if they have issued the documents. This is because if the condition of the property is poor or unsafe you just need to put your complaint to the landlord in writing and they have to reply within 14 days indicating what steps they will be taking to address the complaint.

This means that with issues such as damp, mould, excess cold, electrical hazards, fire risk and serious structural problems, if they **don't reply within 14 days you can complain to the local authority about the same issue.** It will then issue an improvement or emergency remedial notice to the landlord. #snookered

Negotiation

If you think it's right and fair to pay someone exactly what they are asking for, or that it's not worth quibbling over a few quid, then please fast forward to the next chapter, don't pass Go and do not collect £200.

You will be leaving uni with a large debt. How long did you calculate it would take to pay back? It's surely better for money to stay in your account rather than being transferred like a blood transfusion into someone else's.

Typical of a northerner, I don't like giving it away, so I hope you greatly benefit from the contents of this chapter, as we identify some of the issues that need explaining. Then, in the section Profit Maximising, I will discuss tactics that are used to 'transfuse' or 'phish' money from the unwary tenant.

Before we start our expedition to the 'dark side' in the Profit Maximising section, we'll look at a civilised way to negotiate.

To negotiate the best deal for you and/or your housemates, you'll need to be organised and have thought it all through beforehand. The objective of negotiating is to get as much for as little as you can. However, if the other party subsequently thinks they have lost then that could leave them wanting to pull a fast one on you at some other time in order to get even. So they have to feel they have gained something positive. To use management speak, it's not a 'zero-sum' game, i.e. win-lose, it's a 'win-win,' so it's best to leave something in the deal for the other person as well as yourself.

The negotiating process that I was taught in my corporate life was to write down all the points that you think are flexible using the acronym MIL.

Make a list of the issues under the following headings:

a) Must – these are essential items that cannot be compromised over.

b) Intend – these are the additional items that are likely to be agreed upon.

c) Like – these are the items that you aren't expecting, but would like to get included. They are a bit of a try-on, and it would be a great result to get them. E.g. free utilities, unlimited broadband, Sky package with a smart, flat screen 42" TV with surround sound included.

List all the items that need fixing. Do this in writing. Those that are imperative before you move in are the legal and safety issues, e.g.:

✓ Carbon monoxide detector

✓ Location of smoke detector

✓ Loose stair carpet

Signing

Under no circumstances should you sign for accommodation that you haven't seen and inspected thoroughly.

Before signing, highlight any repairs or improvements you would like within the property. Don't be unreasonably demanding by presenting them with a list detailing trivial smears on windows and tiles or a dead fly in the sink, as you want them to choose you as tenants. You will need a good relationship with your landlord otherwise they will only do the bare minimum for you, or less. However, there will be items that you'll need to have fixed before you move in, so get a commitment that these will be taken care of. If you leave this or don't get it in writing then – strangely enough – it's unlikely the items will be fixed. If they don't fix them at this point it's virtually certain they won't fix anything else once you move in (or at least until you threaten to report them).

The best way to ensure that vital repairs/improvements are carried out is to add another clause to the agreement stating, *"Subject to completion of the repairs on the attached list..."*

This means that if the landlord *hasn't fixed these issues by the time you move in then they will be in breach of contract, and should the property be uninhabitable they would be liable to pay for alternative accommodation.*

If the landlord doesn't agree to this clause then you have to understand why not. There may be a valid reason, but maybe they really don't want to do the work, in which case you should consider looking for another property and a different landlord.

Also, don't be afraid of deleting clauses that you don't agree with.

 In addition, *try to get all your housemates together for signing.* Once you have signed the agreement, you are committed to pay the full rent for the full term so you don't want to sign only to be told by one of your housemates that they are changing their mind…

Financials

You will need to clarify:

→ Who is responsible for paying each of the bills, e.g. water, sewage (these are frequently different bills), electricity, gas, insurance, TV licence and broadband.

→ Any other fees the agent has previously specified that you may have to pay, including how much deposit (usually four-weeks' rent).

→ When the property is available and how many months the rental is for (ideally just from September to July).

The financial side of things can seem daunting, but I cover it in detail in Chapter 9. It's important that no one gets lumbered with debt incured by non-paying roommates - so it's important to get all of this clearly set out, before you take on any financial responsibility.

CHAPTER EIGHT

Documentation

Figure 13 - However daunting, read the documentation

Tenancy Agreement!

If it's *confirmed* that you can have the accommodation, there will be a **tenancy agreement** to sign, but don't feel rushed into putting your signature on this straight away, as you need to read it and understand the clauses first. Don't be surprised if an agent tries to scare you by saying that if you don't sign it straight away then someone else will get the property. It's unlikely and it's far better for you to understand the document before signing because a mistake can be VERY costly.

The tenancy agreement is a written contract between you and your landlord (or an authorised third party).

It's not sensible just to sign it because you think it's a standard document that everyone accepts and signs. There are no standard documents and many people make mistakes. Some agreements have lots of conditions that protect the landlord AND the tenant. Some are one-sided and usually contain unfair clauses that will hinder you, but more on that later.

Be aware that some landlords, notably inexperienced ones who are probably fearful of the cost of solicitors in preparing a document, don't provide an Agreement – they are happy to simply verbally agree the terms. **This is a mistake for them and you.**

Do not rent a property without a Rental Agreement, as you are leaving yourself open and could be taken advantage of financially. The agreement is intended to protect BOTH parties.

Agents and landlord's agreements vary in quality and can be very superficial, cover few points and be open to interpretation. **Ambiguity needs to be avoided** because if there is a dispute and you end up in court, it means solicitors will have to interpret, and their time is painfully expensive. However, there is a lot of protection for you; you just need to know what it is.

Unfortunately, many contracts are full of unpunctuated legal speak, which seems to have been written in the time of quill pens and pigeon post, so you may need to reread sentences several times. I know I am repeating myself but it's really important, so you must ask questions. The chances are the landlord or agent doesn't understand it either, in which case they will need it explaining too!

Tenant Rights

You will be pleased to know that you have certain rights throughout your tenancy that protect you and your housemates. Sadly, most tenants – not just students – are unaware of these and many landlords aren't either, so we will cover some of the related issues.

On the agreement itself:

→ **Essential Terms**

These are Essential Terms that MUST be communicated to a tenant, even if there is no written tenancy agreement:

a) **Tenancy's commencement date.**

b) **The Term**. These are usually for a fixed period, and for most students this is usually for between nine and 12 months, so make sure that yours fit to your full academic year (you may want to vacate at the beginning of August). This way they cannot change any of the terms or increase your rent during your academic year without your agreement.

c) **The rents and the period of payment** must be clearly stated.

d) **The landlord's address** (or an address where notices can be served on them, which must be in England or Wales).

It is a criminal offence if they don't provide this information within 28 days of a written request.

At the end of the agreement, there needs to be a section for you and all your housemates to sign, as well as the landlord or letting agent. Some may even have a space for the signature of an independent person as a witness to your signatures, although these days this isn't apparently necessary.

→ **Additional clauses**

In addition, a tenancy agreement is likely to contain clauses relating to the following:

✓ **The deposit to be paid.**

✓ **Use of the property,** i.e. private residential dwelling.

✓ **Description of the property.** If the rental is for a room in a shared accommodation then the description needs to be specific, e.g. front bedroom, left-hand side, bedroom on third floor, entry via second door on the right-hand side on landing. It's even better if the bedrooms are numbered or named.

✓ **Payments other than rent**, e.g. council tax, water and sewerage charges, utilities, telephone, broadband.

✓ **Repairs and redecoration, including appliances.**

✓ **Damage and alterations**, e.g. changing locks. Regarding locks, you need to be aware that landlords do not have the automatic right to hold a key for the duration of the tenancy.

✓ **Access and inspections.**

✓ **Assignment and subletting** (it's sensible for a landlord to prohibit these as they are likely to contravene their mortgage terms).

✓ **Insurance.**

✓ **Forfeiture.** This relates to evicting a tenant during the fixed term under specific circumstances, e.g. if rent isn't paid for 21 days. This needs to comply with legislation, so it's most likely to be an unenforceable term.

✓ **Prohibitions.** For example, smoking, keeping pets, storing inflammable liquids, keeping illegal substances.

→ **Penalty clauses**

These may relate to the following:

✓ Penalty for non-payment of rent.

✓ Claiming interest on unpaid rent (4% above the bank rate is typical, but if it's higher it's probably unreasonable so is unlikely to be enforceable).

✓ Missed appointment.

✓ Administration expenses.

✓ Charges when a letter is sent out.

✓ Charge if a rental payment is made by cash or cheque, i.e. not automatically by the bank.

✓ Noise (e.g. playing of musical instruments between 11:00pm and 7:00am).

The good news for you is that you have **plenty of legal protection,** although most tenants aren't aware of this.

The Unfair Terms in Consumer Contracts Regulations 1999 states that a standard term is unfair if it creates a significant imbalance in the parties' rights and obligations under the contract, to the detriment of the consumer, and contrary to the requirement of good faith.

The regulations also require that plain and intelligible language is used and a term is open to challenge if it is difficult to understand by an 'ordinary person' (as stated earlier, the reality is that many agreements are not in plain English, but defining this is subjective).

The additional good news for you is that many terms found in rental agreements can in fact be contrary to the requirement of good faith and are to the detriment of the consumer.

The Office of Fair Trading has produced a somewhat lengthy explanatory document specifically relating to tenancy agreements, so if you have any concerns about the wording of your Agreement or the actions of your landlord or agent, look up www.gov.uk and search for 'Unfair terms in rental agreement'

The document itself is surprisingly helpful, although the index is inadequate. It's also clearly written and does cover many issues. If you have any disputes at the end of your tenancy, simply referring the landlord to the appropriate section could save you a lot of money from recharges.

There are so many examples of unfair terms that I would just *download it* and have a quick read through so that you understand what clauses are likely to be unfair and therefore unenforceable.

A few examples:

a) If an agent or landlord has clauses in their contract that refer you to some small print that is located elsewhere, then unless they provide you with that information/document then the clause will be unenforceable. See Group 9 ref 3.80 p.32.

b) Fair Wear and Tear (FWAT). Landlords frequently expect to have their property vacated and left in the same condition as when the tenants moved in. This is misinformation. As a result of FWAT, a landlord is not entitled to demand professional cleaning and redecoration. He is expected to receive it back in a clean and tidy condition. See Group 18 4.8 p.50.

c) Rights of Entry to the Property. A tenant is allowed 'exclusive possession' and 'quiet enjoyment' of the property during the tenancy. See 3.32 p.18.

d) Many of the penalty clauses stated previously will also be deemed to be unfair. See Group 5 3.44 p.21.

e) Tenants' property left after departure. If there is a clause relating to this, refer to Group 18c 4.19 p.54. There is a process that needs to be followed.

In fact, it's so important go and download it now!

The Consumer Protection from Unfair Trading Regulations 2008 also applies to rented properties. (The Property Misdescriptions Act 1991, which many people refer to, was repealed in 2013, as the principles are covered by the Consumer Protection Regulations above.)

So, it's important that all statements made by the landlord and letting agent **are true**. If they are not, then a tenant may be able to claim for misrepresentation, cancel the agreement and claim back any money paid.

Moving in Date

Some landlords may insist you move in during August. However, many accept that they won't get any rent for this month and use the time to complete repairs and to do a bit of redecorating. However, this won't stop them asking for it to be paid.

Negotiate your start and leaving dates in order to reduce your rental payments.

If they insist you pay for August, then tell them that you've seen other properties where rent for this month isn't expected. If you really like the property, *you can always then ask them for a reduced rent or for them to throw in free broadband or utility bills.*

Keys

It's essential that *every housemate has a set of keys*. Every tenant who is named on an AST MUST be given the appropriate entrance keys.

Do not let the agent or landlord try to tell you that it's your responsibility to get keys cut. It can get expensive! A set of keys for each tenant is their responsibility.

They should photograph the keys they give you and include these in the inventory.

If they are being difficult, politely remind them that if you have to get a key cut, *you will retain the key* (which means they will have to go to great expense and inconvenience to replace the lock(s) when you vacate).

CHAPTER NINE

Payments - Rent & Bills

Deposits

The landlord has the right to ask you for a deposit before you move in. The reason for this is that it gives the landlord some protection against any damage or unpaid rent or bills. It is a reasonable request. The amount of the deposit is likely to be four to eight weeks' rent.

However, please note that…

> …with an AST, the deposit must be protected with a government-approved scheme within 30 days of being paid. You should be given the Deposit Protection Certificate and Prescribed Information for Tenants within 30 days of payment. If this does not happen the landlord may be unable to withhold any of your deposit at the end of the tenancy. Not only that, but you could take them to court and they could be forced to pay you compensation!

The amount of the deposit is negotiable, so it's in your interest to get the amount reduced, even if it's just to four-weeks' rent. Also bear in mind that as a result of the above deposit scheme, a number of landlords have found it easier NOT to ask for one, so you may get lucky.

If you can't afford the deposit then you can ask your local authority's housing department or housing advice centre whether there is a rent or deposit guarantee scheme, which will guarantee rent or damage cost for a certain period of time.

There is more information about deposits and what they cover on page 118, including the types of schemes in place to protect them.

Notice to quit

A 'Section 21' form gives the landlord the authority to terminate the AST at the end of the term on your Agreement (not earlier), so that the AST doesn't rollover into a Statutory Periodic Tenancy and therefore commit them to giving you another two months' notice. However, once issued, a Section 21 must be enforced within six months or it is invalid. A landlord cannot enforce this notice without a court order.

Many landlords had these signed at the start of a tenancy but this changed in 2015. Section 21 notices are now supposed to be signed on a date that is four months after your AST is dated (in September 2016 I am still seeing agents' websites that have not been updated). If you are asked to sign one at the start of the tenancy then they have not been updated on legislation and the Section 21 is unenforceable.

If a Section 21 notice isn't issued at the end of the tenancy, you do not have to leave the property until two months after the notice has been issued.

Paying Rent

This section covers the things that you need to know in making your payments throughout the term of your tenancy.

Monthly or four weekly payments?

Usually, rent is paid on a *calendar month basis*. However, as local councils frequently make housing benefit payments on a four weekly basis, you need to ensure that your tenancy agreement is not one that was designed for housing benefit tenants, otherwise you will have to make 13 payments during the course of a 12-month year.

Rent increases

The rent should be a fixed amount for the duration of the tenancy and both the amount, start and end dates should be stated in the tenancy agreement. If there is a clause allowing rent to be increased then delete it.

The terms of your Rental Agreement remain unless you and the landlord both agree (in writing!) to any changes.

In many towns and cities where there is a high student population, it's common for rental values to increase due to high demand. When extending your tenancy into the next academic year, if your landlord is trying to increase the rent be prepared to look around for somewhere else. Do some research – it's easy to do online and it will only take 15 minutes to get a decent overview.

If you see somewhere similar, preferably close by but cheaper, show it to the agent or landlord and negotiate their price back down.

Payment methods

The best way to pay your rent is by setting up an automated payment by direct debit or standing order.

Some landlords accept cheques or bank transfers when rent is due. This may seem convenient and give you control, but it will waste both yours and the landlord's time and can end up in a disagreement if you don't keep full, signed records or the payment isn't quickly cleared by the bank. In addition, some agencies and landlords charge a fee if the rent has to be collected (and then taken to the bank), is not received on time, or they have to process cheques (sometimes the banks will also charge business customers for banking cheques).

For budgeting purposes, some students **set up a separate bank account for their rent, utilities and living expenses** to ensure they don't spend this essential money on day-to-day items or entertainment. So, if you feel you may be less than disciplined in your attitude to money, it's worth considering an additional account.

Remember that if you **fail to pay your rent** it can affect your right to remain in the property, and some landlords will also make a surcharge for late payments plus the additional administration time it takes to chase you.

The difference between a Standing Order (SO) and a Direct Debit (DD) is that *with a standing order you are the only person who can change the date or payment amount.* With a *direct debit, the person or company you are paying can change these details.* This is important – you have control with a SO. With a DD the amount can increase without your confirmation.

The payment is automatically made and deducted from your bank account on a specific date. It is important that your account has sufficient funds to allow for payment otherwise you could be faced with an additional charge.

Struggling to pay your rent?

In difficult circumstances, tenants can seek support and request help from housing benefit – www.gov.uk/housing-benefit/how-to-claim. The landlord can assist you with this, helping you submit a valid housing benefit form. However, the landlord has the obligation to terminate the tenancy if rental payments are regularly late. Also, please note that (currently) the **vast majority of undergraduates cannot claim housing benefit.**

> **If you cannot pay your rent or you decide that you have had enough and want to return home prior to the end of the tenancy, your rent for the whole tenancy period is still payable.**

If one of your housemates has this problem then you need to make sure that they continue to pay up, as all the signatories on the agreement are liable for the full amount of the rent specified in the agreement.

Guarantor

It's very likely that you will be asked to *provide a guarantor*. They are important because without one it's unlikely you'll be able to rent a property due to the fact you won't have a regular income. This section explains what they are and what they have to do.

What is a Guarantor?

A guarantor is someone who agrees to be responsible for a tenant's rental payments and contractual obligations within a tenancy agreement in the event that the tenant is unable to make the payment. This means: **if you don't pay your rent, the guarantor will have to.**

A guarantor *isn't legally required* and it is ultimately the landlord's decision to request one in order for the tenancy to go ahead. However, most landlords and letting agents do require one for extra financial security when dealing with student lets.

So, should the tenant default on their rental payments and/or fail to pay for any damage caused to the property, the landlord may take both the tenant and the guarantor to court for the shortfall in payments.

The guarantor is usually a parent, but needs to be a UK resident, and it's preferable if you choose somebody who is employed. If they aren't then there is a good chance their guarantee won't be accepted and you will have to find someone else anyway. Do ensure you ask your potential guarantor if they would be happy to act as one before you put a document in front of their nose!

There are different types of guarantee given, so everyone signing the contract needs to understand exactly what they are committing to.

→ **Guarantor forms**

This is a legal contract stating that the guarantor **accepts responsibility for any contractual monies owed to the landlord by the tenant.** In short, if the tenant defaults the guarantor has to pay. If the guarantor refuses to pay then he is likely to end up in court.

The guarantor form can be included in the tenancy agreement or it can also be written as a separate document. However, on a technical point, it must be signed BEFORE the AST.

✓ In tenancy agreements

This may contain additional clause(s) that deal with the guarantor and set out their liability. In this case, the guarantor will also need to sign the tenancy agreement and any subsequent amendment to the agreement.

✓ As a separate document

This is a separate legal contract between the landlord and the guarantor that sets out the terms and conditions. The following should be noted:

a) The document containing the guarantee must make specific reference to the tenant and the tenancy agreement between the landlord and the tenant.

b) The landlord should provide the guarantor with a copy of the tenancy agreement so he/she is aware of the provisions that are contained in the agreement.

c) If at any point a new tenancy agreement is created between the tenant and the landlord, the landlord will need the guarantor to sign a new guarantee and, as with the original guarantor form, it must be signed BEFORE the new AST.

The landlord will also need to be confident that should the tenant default on payments **the guarantor can make them.** Therefore, the guarantor may also be required to supply proof of identity such as a passport/driving licence and proof of income, e.g. a bank statement or salary slips. The guarantor will need to sign a document to confirm their permission for a credit reference to be taken.

Many guarantors believe they are guaranteeing the rent for their own son/daughter/relative. Unfortunately, in many cases, it's a wider responsibility than this. Many guarantor forms state a 'joint and several liability'. **In other words, the guarantor is providing a guarantee for the WHOLE of the rent on the agreement, not just one student's.**

So, in order to provide a guarantee for just your payments, it's recommended that your guarantor specifies on the form their name, the period of tenancy and the total amount to be guaranteed.

This means that if your rent is £280 per month for 11 months, then the total liability is £3,080 and not the total rent due for the whole property.

The landlord or agent may also ask for the guarantor's phone number and email address. This isn't for marketing purposes, as an organised agent will simply send the guarantor a copy of any communication if you are behind with your payments.

As a point of note, as the landlord and/or agent will be holding information on tenants and guarantors (effectively a database), they must be registered annually for the appropriate categories with the Information Commissioners Office (ICO).

Deposit

There are a couple of payments that agents or landlords will want you to make when you are signing all the paperwork, so let's take a look at these. I'll include some of the more 'questionable' ones in the 'profit maximising' section on page 122.

Damage/security/dilapidation deposit

This is the amount of money paid upfront that is retained against your account until your departure and used to offset any damages that have occurred. **It must be protected within 30 days of payment.**

This deposit is the most contentious aspect of any rental and is the area where you are most likely to have a dispute with the landlord.

However, most tenants don't realise how much protection they have, so read about this in the next chapter.

A couple of points relating to deposits:

✓ It's not a legal requirement to take a deposit and some landlords choose not to request them, although in the student market these are few and far between.

✓ Deposits are unlikely to be for more than two months' rent, otherwise it will be deemed in law to be a "premium" for the landlord or agent. New legislation is planned that will state two months' rent as the maximum deposit.

What are tenancy deposit protection schemes?

In England and Wales, if you rent your home on an Assured Shorthold Tenancy, your landlord (or agent) must place your deposit in an approved tenancy deposit protection (TDP) scheme. Having stated this, the legislation doesn't apply to student accommodation that is let directly by universities or colleges.

It's worth pointing out that your landlord or agent doesn't have to protect a **holding deposit** (see page 124), as this is a different type of deposit. However, once you become a tenant, the holding deposit will become a 'security' or 'dilapidation' deposit, which they must protect.

In addition, your deposit must be protected in a scheme even if someone else pays it, which will most likely be your parents. Don't let an agent tell you otherwise. Any third party that has contributed to the deposit must also be given the deposit protection documents within 30 days.

At the date of writing, there are three approved schemes:

→ Deposit Protection Service (Custodial and Insured)

→ mydeposits

→ Tenancy Deposit Scheme

These government-backed schemes are compulsory and will ensure you will have your deposit handled fairly, without the landlord taking unjustified deductions, as long as you:

✓ Meet the terms of your tenancy agreement.

✓ Don't damage the property.

✓ Pay your rent and bills.

The schemes also provide a free dispute resolution service (arbitration) in the event of a disagreement between tenant and landlord over the amount of the deposit being returned.

Landlords or the agents working on their behalf MUST protect your deposit in accordance with the rules of the tenancy deposit scheme.

Your money is therefore safe (i.e. nobody can run off with it) provided the rules of the scheme are followed. You therefore need to ensure the agent/landlord is following the rules and **get a receipt for your deposit** (the amount of your deposit should also be stated within your tenancy agreement).

You have a LOT of leverage to ensure they comply. If they or the agent working on their behalf fails to protect your deposit within 30 days from the date of receipt, **they can face a fine of up to three times the amount of the deposit.**

In addition, they would not be able to gain possession of the accommodation by using the usual section 21 notice of the Housing Act 1988 (which they would otherwise need to use for the end of your tenancy), unless the deposit was returned before issuing the notice.

In addition, within 30 days of receiving a deposit, the landlord or agent must give the tenant details about how their deposit is protected, including 'prescribed information'.

This includes:

- ✓ The address of the rented property.
- ✓ How much deposit you've paid.
- ✓ How the deposit is protected.
- ✓ The name and contact details of the tenancy deposit protection (TDP) scheme and its dispute resolution service.
- ✓ Their (or the letting agency's) name and contact details.
- ✓ The name and contact details of any third party that has paid the deposit.
- ✓ Details of how they would keep some or all of the deposit.
- ✓ How to apply to get the deposit back.
- ✓ What to do if you can't get hold of the landlord at the end of the tenancy.

✓   What to do if there's a dispute over the deposit.

All this information should be contained within documents that have been provided to the landlord or agent. As the tenant you will have to confirm receipt of this information.

Deductions to deposits after the tenancy

It's important to know that the tenant must be given proof of costs related to deductions/stoppages and the amount of the undisputed sum within 10 working days of the end of the tenancy. If there is then a dispute over the amount deducted you'll need to follow the arbitration rules of the scheme in which your deposit is protected.

The schemes work in two different ways:

→ **Custodial** - this is where the landlord or agent has to hand your deposit over to the scheme administrators. The Deposit Protection Service will handle this.

→ **Insurance backed schemes** – this is where the agent or landlord retains the deposit while it is registered with the scheme. If there is a dispute, you simply contact the scheme's administrators.

Once you've agreed the amount of deposit to be returned to you (if it's an insurance-backed scheme), you'll be paid the money directly. The landlord will need to inform the scheme how much is being returned to you, for which you should get a notification so that you can confirm it. If it's a custodial scheme, then the administrators will be advised and you will be refunded by the scheme. In both cases, the agreed refund has to be made within 10 days of notification.

If, however, you have a disagreement with the landlord the dispute can be referred to the scheme's independent arbitrators. In an insurance-based scheme, your deposit then has to be transferred by the landlord or agent to the administrators, where it will be held until the issue(s) is resolved and the arbitrator has made a judgement regarding how much of the deposit should be returned. Both parties have to agree to the use of the arbitrator, although it can be resolved by the County Court. However, this is more time-consuming.

The arbitrators will usually make their decision without a hearing, basing it on the written details provided by both parties. So, if you end up going down this route, ensure you provide all the facts and evidence including (dated) photographs and copies of relevant paperwork.

Ten days after notification of the judgement, the deposit money will be returned as ordered.

Information relating to deposit refund disputes is provided in the later section on 'Deposit Refunds'.

Profit Maximising

We have now reached the Dark Side. It's where previously agreeable, friendly agents develop horns, long claws and cannot resist making a grab for your cash. So, with the benefit of night-vision goggles, we will see what happens in the Dark Side.

Figure 14 - Keeping out the money demons.

The agent's terms of business contain the hidden extras. Some are valid but others are manufactured in order to inflate their profit, or, if you look at it another way, to make their business viable.

 Always ask for a copy of their terms of business at an early stage so you can read it when you have time to scrutinise it, rather than being rushed.

Payment terms

Many student tenancies are based on rent per week and payment can be required either weekly, monthly, calendar monthly or each term in advance. However, you need to ensure you understand the actual cost so you can compare the true total costs of different properties over the whole tenancy period. For instance, make sure that if your tenancy agreement states payments are on a calendar month basis, you do not pay on a four week basis, as this would result in 13 payments per year.

Service charges

It is normal for service charges to be paid by a landlord to the freeholder, usually when it's a block of flats and there are communal costs, e.g. electric, light and heat, replacement of carpets, lift or roof repairs. This is a cost that should be included within your rent, so make sure that a separate charge isn't being made.

Finder's fee

Some letting agencies charge a fee for finding the property that a tenant chooses to rent.

Don't accept this. This is a basic element of their job, as they are paid by the landlord to find a tenant. It should therefore be a free service. Be wary of an agent using this tactic because if they try to pull this one off, they are sure to try others.

Don't pay a finder's fee to an agent, except in the unlikely instance there are no other properties available through other ones. Expect this fee to become illegal when the new legislation is confirmed.

Pre-tenancy agreement/reservation fee/holding deposit

These are fixed amounts of money that a tenant agrees to pay in advance of the tenancy start date to secure the accommodation, and they are non-refundable. The reason for these is to stop the accommodation being let to anyone else.

This appears commercially reasonable and in my opinion it's only fair that they ask you for a reservation fee as they need to complete credit checks on you and they should also take the property off the market. If they do this and you change your mind about the property they have not only had their time wasted but they may have missed an opportunity to rent the property to someone else. This could actually cost them a month's rent.

Unfortunately, especially in London, a number of agents make this fee extortionate.

Nevertheless, as previously referred to, the government is looking to **ban agents' fees to tenants.** In my opinion this is harsh on agents because we should all show more respect for others' time. In this case, an agent's time is what an economist would call an 'opportunity cost'. In other words, they could have invested their time in something productive. I hope that instead of banning it they set a maximum fee.

---

*So...*only agree to the fee if it will become part of your first rental payment should you start the tenancy, with the additional caveat you will get a refund if a failure to start the tenancy is outside of your control, i.e. it's the fault of the agent or landlord. Write this on their documentation before you sign it.

Retainer fees

To keep the accommodation over the summer break if your tenancy is, for example, nine months (the academic year), you may wish to pay a retainer fee over the summer period to keep the property available to rent the following academic year.

Again, this is reasonable and is considerably better than paying additional months at full rent. Whatever they ask for, try to negotiate a lower fee. If you aren't confident about asking, let me reassure you that it's easier than you think and you don't have to be hard-faced. Just say it's more than you were expecting to pay, so can they reduce it.

Also, their fees need to be capped otherwise they will be in breach of the Unfair Contract Terms regulations.

Fee retention should be no more than the number of days they've not been able to market the property as a result of you pulling out.

To estimate a reasonable charge, say it's a week's delay, it would therefore be a week's rent plus an inflated £25 for an hour of their time. See Unfair Terms in 'Consumer Contracts Regulations 1999' Group 6 3.66 p.27.

Administration fees

These are regularly charged and the amounts vary and are frequently non-refundable. In principle, all fees should be paid by their client, the landlord. However, if all the agents in an area charge the same amount it makes it more difficult to negotiate, so this type of fee is usually found where the agents in an area have low charges to landlords. It's a bit like when low-cost airlines add booking fees or charge for seat selection so they can advertise the low, net cost of the flight. You can, of course, be mischievous and confidently ask them what service they are providing for this fee, then say you don't see why you should pay it. See how they react.

I have heard of agents charging £500 without any idea what administration they actually do when it comes to setting up a rental agreement for a landlord – let alone for a tenant – to actually justify this amount.

If an agent asks for this fee then you can simply blag it and say that other agents you've spoken to are happy to waive this if the tenancy goes ahead. You can also ask them how long it takes to complete the administration. Then assume they are paid £25 per hour (£200 per day, the same as an expensive tradesman outside London) and see what the cost will be. They have maybe an hour's work to do on your behalf in checking references, sending out documentation and making phone calls.

Nevertheless, you have on your side the Unfair Terms in Consumer Contracts Regulations 1999, which provides you with protection should you wish to dispute the fee.

So, if the polite method doesn't persuade them to make the fee a reasonable amount (e.g. £25) you can take a more assertive approach and quote the above statute before suggesting again that they need to review it before you complete the admin.

I hope and indeed expect this fee not to be allowed in the forthcoming legislation.

Referencing fee

If you are paying an administration fee then this should include the reference checks.

However, it's unjustifiable if your agent is trying to charge for separate references as well.

In the main, agents only complete a basic reference check so it should cost less than £20.

Again, this fee will be reviewed in the planned legislation and I hope it will not be allowed because it's a cost that should be paid by the landlord.

Several years ago, I had a tenant whose previous agent had (outrageously) withheld their holding deposit because they didn't pass the credit check. Despite my advice, the tenants just accepted it and lost £500. The cliché, "you can lead a horse..." comes to mind.

Withholding the whole deposit when their costs have been approximately £30 for a single credit check and three days of lost marketing isn't financially justifiable. So, until there is new legislation, refer to the Unfair Terms in Consumer Contracts Regulations 1999.

In addition, if the retention of the deposit is as a result of a poor reference, you should also ask for a copy of it. The agent may try to bluff you by stating it contravenes the Data Protection Act. That is not true.

The agent is working on your behalf so the references are yours.

If they don't have a written reference and it was done over the phone then ask for one in writing or contact the referee and double check whether they gave one. If they did, ask them to put whatever they said in writing for you.

A credit check will cost less than £30, so it's not acceptable for an agent to charge more than this or to retain your whole deposit if your credit is declined.

In instances like this, it's possible that the agent has found another tenant and is trying to use this as an opportunity to misappropriate your deposit.

If they resist returning your fees then tell them you will take them to court.

It's not difficult (although it can be time-consuming) and it's bad publicity for the agent to be taken to court. Don't forget how important their reputation is to them. Be prepared to threaten the agent in writing, even if you don't want to go to court yourself. Being assertive is more likely to get them to back down. They are playing chicken. Don't let them try to defer you.

Also, some agents have been known to charge the fee to each tenant. Again, if this amounts to more than £30 per person, including a credit check, and as it will take up maybe 30 minutes of their time, a higher fee can't be justified. So resist it. Go and check on Rightmove – www.rightmove.co.uk – to see if there is another agent marketing the property and check their terms of business. You can always rent through another agent.

The replies to the credit checks should be returned and completed within three days.

Inventory fee

The fee for an inventory should be paid by the landlord. It's their property.

Some agents charge the landlord for a check-in inventory and the tenants for the check-out one. This may seem fairer, but the landlord is the client, so they should pay for both. In some cases the agent is pulling a fast one and charging the landlord AND the tenant. This practice is known as "double-dipping".

If it isn't completed then the landlord cannot expect to go to the arbitrator in a dispute over any deductions for damages because they will lose. If one is completed, you will have to sign the document for it to be used in arbitration, so you will be entitled to a copy.

However, if the landlord doesn't have an inventory completed I would certainly complete a full one myself with photos. However, if you are not sure what you are doing, you should be able to get one completed for approximately £60 (it will be more if it's an HMO as there will be communal areas) and it's better to pay that than to get accused of having damaged the property or its contents, which will be time-consuming to dispute.

Deposit protection fee

Landlords have to pay a fee to register the compulsory tenancy deposit.

Currently they can charge you for this. It will be approximately £30 in total, not per tenant. To make sure that neither the landlord nor the agent have inflated the amount they have paid, ask them for a copy of the invoice.

Tenancy renewal fee

This is an unnecessary profit maximiser and I hope it will become illegal. However, in the meantime...

...if you see this clause showing a tenancy renewal fee delete it from your agreement.

The agent will get paid by the landlord, as they are the client. At worst, negotiate with the landlord if you decide to renew and decide whether the landlord is looking to increase his rent. If you have been good tenants and agree to stay another year you will save the landlord a lot of hassle and worry. If you tell the agent you will move elsewhere, as they will probably get a fee from the landlord, they may back down.

Renewal credit checks

Greedy profit maximiser

Delete renewal credit checks from your Agreement before you sign it. It's a fee that needs to become illegal.

Inspection fee

An inspection of the property is to be expected after approximately six months, but this is for the landlord's benefit. **If they want to charge a tenant for this then it's another shameless profit maximiser to be deleted from your Agreement and made illegal.**

Key cutting

The agreement may specify that if you lose a key they will charge you a specific amount of money to get a replacement. I've heard of £150 being charged. **This is outright greed.**

A standard Yale type key should cost £4 – £6 for a (larger) mortice key. Add on half an hour's labour and it's less than £30. If there is a break-in and they have to replace the door lock then £100 is realistic.

Either delete the clause from the agreement prior to signing it, or, if you decide not to delete it but then experience such an incident, don't pay a substantial fee. Again, this would come under the Unfair Contract Terms regulations, so you can dispute it if it's deducted from your deposit.

Utility maintenance

As previously described, the responsibility for equipment servicing and electrical and gas safety checks is down to the landlord. Testing the fire alarm is something you will be expected to carry out and you should replace the battery if it's not a mains powered one.

Any clause in the agreement that tries to pass this responsibility and cost to the tenant is illegal, so you can either delete it or ignore any demands for payment.

Replacing light bulbs and batteries

These are consumables so it is fair that *you pay for them*. Therefore, you will need to replace these if there is a clause in the agreement that states this. When you initially inspect the property you should check that all the bulbs are working and get the landlord to agree in writing to replace any that aren't. Non-LED downlighters (e.g. GU10s) have a tendency not to last and they can be comparatively expensive and awkward to replace.

As there are a number of items that you will be responsible for,I have added a document listing these in the downloads section of the website

 www.smartstudentguides.com/bookdocs

I give this document for tenants to sign so that they understand the rules of the house. It covers what types of light bulbs are needed, where to find the stopcock, and cleaning, etc. In fact, while chatting with an award-winning letting agent (Castledene Property Management – www.castledene.co.uk) I discovered they have a handout for their tenants called *'Tenants' Repair Obligations'*. As it ensures clarity, I feel this should be provided by every agent and landlord. Thanks John, I have now improved my own document.

As some modern fittings need a special tool with which to remove the bulb or its holder, it's worth finding out if you'll need any of these when checking the property.

 Take a photo of the type of bulbs you'll need on your smart phone, then when you're at the supermarket you'll know exactly what to buy.

Fridge or washing machine failure

You may be charged for repairing a white goods break down. This is only fair if it's definitely your fault, although fridges seldom break down.

However, if the appliance needs replacing do not accept having to pay for it.

Washing machines tend to last five to 10 years, depending on usage, but I cannot imagine what you would have done to seriously injure a fridge, so I would guess that any repairs required are as a result of wear and tear over time.

In this case, most of the wear and tear is probably from previous use. The most you should have to pay is a pro-rata percentage based on your length of usage against the total age of the machine.

It's not acceptable for your tenancy agreement to state that it's your responsibility to replace any broken appliances and nor would I be happy to pay for repairs. I recommend you delete the clause and discuss it with the agent or landlord. The landlord is responsible for these items and ensuring they work. It's fair enough to pay if the breakdown is your fault, but you shouldn't be paying for wear and tear as a result of previous usage.

If the appliance is seven years old and it breaks down after you have been living there for three months, and it would cost £200 to replace, then you should pay no more than the pro-rata number of months that you have been responsible for the appliance. In this case 3/84ths, which would only be £7.15!

Waste removal surcharge

Recently, some councils tried to charge landlords for the collection of waste from student rental accommodation. They justified it under the Controlled Waste (England and Wales) Regulations 2012 by extending the definition of "businesses that provide self-catering accommodation" to include student accommodation. This was a money-grabbing surcharge (thousands of pounds), which would have undoubtedly resulted in students being additionally charged by the landlord.

The good news is that in August 2013, the National Landlords Association confirmed the government had informed them that the legislation does NOT apply to student accommodation.

If you get charged for waste removal as a result of a council surcharge then politely ask for a copy of their invoice from the council.

That should suffice as a deterrent. If they do provide an invoice, I suggest you refuse to pay it and tell them to take it up with the council, as it's not authorised to charge them. Tell them they should also speak to the National Landlords Association (or another body they belong to) to get advice.

Do you want to make a complaint about any fees?

Initially, you must complain directly to the agent or landlord, and confirm this in writing (obviously you need to keep a copy and make sure that it's dated). If it's through a letting agent and they don't resolve the issue within eight weeks, or they don't have a complaints procedure, take your complaint to a letting agent redress scheme – all agents must be a member of one.

See: www.theprs.co.uk/propertyagent/who-needs-to-join.

If your agent doesn't belong to a redress scheme or the fees are unlawful then you can complain to the local council's trading standards department through a Citizens Advice Bureau. It is a criminal offence for a letting agent not to be a member of a redress scheme, and a local council can issue a fixed penalty fine, which at the time of writing is up to £5000. This gives you plenty of leverage to get things agreed.

The three government-approved letting agent redress schemes are:

1. The Property Ombudsman (TPO)

2. The Property Redress Scheme

3. Ombudsman Services Property

Their websites are listed in the spreadsheet of useful websites in the downloads section of
www.smartstudentguides.com/bookdocs

The letting agent must pay you compensation promptly or fix a problem if the redress scheme orders them to do this. You will obviously need to inform the scheme if the agent does not comply.

If the letting agent is a member of a professional association you can also complain to them. To do this you'll need to provide copies of any correspondence with the agent.

General complaint about the agent

In addition, if it's an issue about problems not being solved or attended to, rather than going 'nuclear' you could contact the landlord direct. It's quite possible that he or she won't be aware of the service levels you are receiving from their agent.

Most councils have a Tenancy Relations Officer (TRO), who can help you if your landlord is breaking the law. So, if your landlord threatens to evict you illegally, is harassing you, is failing to carry out repairs or to fix problems relating to gas or fire safety, then the TRO may get involved. Ultimately, they can prosecute the landlord if they ignore their advice.

If there is a health and safety hazard in your home that your landlord has failed to fix despite reminders, then you could make a complaint to the local council's environmental health department. This could cover issues such as a dangerous structural problem, dangerous electrics, faulty gas pipes or appliances, rising damp or leaky roofs, the presence of asbestos, or if the landlord is not complying with HMO rules.

CHAPTER TEN

Making a Home & Protecting Your Deposit

Figure 15 - Looking after the property. Or not!

Well, this is the exciting part. A new home. A new life. There's much to look forward to and at this stage it's so easy to relax and enjoy the warm feelings. FREEDOM!

Think about your conversations with friends who have already had experience of renting. Did any of them NOT get money deducted from their deposit? Thought not. How much money did they lose? How did they feel about the deduction? Was it fair?

So, with that in mind, let's defer the warm feelings until later and return to this commercial world so we can make your life easier, save you money and protect your deposit.

Let's get a grip.

Moving In

There's a moving in checklist on
www.smartstudentguides.com/bookdocs

The checklist covers many of the following points so it might be worthwhile downloading a copy so you can write comments against each one when you move in.

Sometimes you're just given the keys at the letting agent's office, but your agent or landlord should make the time to meet you and show you where everything is, how things work and take meter readings.

As previously stated, it's essential that every housemate has a set of keys. Do not let the agent or landlord pass this off to you, as it may cost each of you £10 just to get a couple of keys made up.

In order to confirm the general condition of the property at handover and ensure any damage is logged, taking notes and snapping pictures will be great evidence in any forthcoming disputes. Inform the letting agent immediately of any damage, or if rubbish or unwanted items you didn't see during the viewing have been left in the property. Take photographs and put it all in writing. **Some inventory clerks suggest that you should take a photo or video of a room with the landlord in it.** Do make sure that your camera puts a date on the photos so it's indisputable. Photos are like a virus checker for your deposit, protecting you from phishing emails that are looking for your bank details.

Remember that once you have the keys, YOU are responsible for the condition of the property.

 Take photos of damage, **preferably whilst the agent/landlord is on the premises**, as these will protect you from your deposit being withheld unfairly.

What to ask?

Use the opportunity to ask questions so you can understand how things work and **where things are located**. It's much better to do this when the landlord or agent is present rather than wasting time looking for answers on your own or facing a flood without knowing how to switch off the water supply!

> **If you didn't get a copy at the time you completed the paperwork, and if the property has gas supplied, ask for a copy of a current Gas Safe certificate. See: www.gassaferegister.co.uk. As previously stated, it's a legal requirement.**

Main questions to ask:

→ **Where are the meter cupboards for gas, electric and water?** You should write down all the meter readings, or, even better, *photograph them with your mobile phone*. You can provide these figures to your utility providers once you've moved in.

→ **What are the current utility suppliers' details and can you change suppliers if you find a cheaper one?**

→ **Where is the stopcock (for switching off the water supply)?** Ensure that it works, as in older properties they regularly seize. This is VERY important because if you suffer a leak you can at least control the size of it by switching the water off at the source.

From personal experience, I can tell you how unpleasant it is to have a pipe burst. Coincidentally this happened when I was close to publishing this book, so this account is a late addition. I was at my girlfriend's flat when a pipe burst under the sink. A connection to the tap had sheared so water was gushing out at high pressure. My girlfriend didn't know where the stopcock was and the water was so hot that not only was the cupboard being sprayed with scalding hot water, but my glasses also steamed up when I got close. I couldn't see a thing and needed to wrap towels around my hand to tolerate the heat.

You can't stop water by putting a towel over it, so after quickly pulling out all the items from the cupboard, we put a couple of bowls inside it to collect the water while I wrapped my arms in a cold towel and searched around for an isolating valve. Thankfully there was one and I managed to close off the supply. This was made more difficult by slapdash plumbing, as the valve was at a daft angle and was difficult to reach with a screwdriver. Grrrr.

It took half an hour to mop up. We just hoped that the water hadn't soaked through the floor into the flat below.

This was all very unpleasant and all because we didn't initially know where the stopcock was located (it was hidden behind boarding in an airing cupboard and no easy access panel had been fitted). Another grrrrrrr.

→ **Where is the consumer unit/fuse board and how do you switch all the electrics off,** or reactivate a trip switch when one cuts out or blows?

→ **Where is the valve to switch off the gas?**

→ Are there **copies of manuals for the appliances** (fridge, washing machine, oven and hob, microwave, etc.), kitchen equipment and heating?

→ **How does the cooker work?** (These can be frustrating, as they sometimes don't work until the clock has been set, so ask for an instruction book.)

→ **How does the heating/hot water operate and how do you increase/reduce the temperature of water and radiators? How do you set the timers?**

→ **How do the showers work?**

→ **How does the extractor work?** (This is important, especially in the bathroom, because if there is no extractor there is likely to be an increase in moisture, resulting in damp, mould and paintwork damage.)

→ **How does the boiler work** (if there is one) and how do you increase pressure if it drops? (This would result in your hot water supply not working.)

→ **How do the window/door locks work and where are the spare keys?** (Double glazed windows that open usually need a key to unlock the handle.)

→ **Which day is the rubbish/recycling collected** and where does it need to be taken?

→ **How do you test the smoke alarms** (and stop them if you overcook your fry-up) and when were the batteries last replaced?

→ **How do you get into the loft** and is it okay to store stuff up there?

→ **Ask when the inventory is being completed,** but do point out any issues that still need fixing or are unsatisfactory.

- *Move the bed and any sets of drawers and inspect the walls behind to make sure there is no mould present.*

- *Note any badly fitting switches, light fittings and shades and ask for these to be fixed.*

→ Again, **ask for a copy of a service level agreement** that the agent may have with the landlord, or ask the landlord if they have a written "rules of the house".

Download the spreadsheet of useful websites at
www.smartstudentguides.com/bookdocs

Also, remember that the landlord's contact details must be displayed in a prominent position so each tenant has access to them.

Inventory/schedule of condition

These are more important than most people realise when they are moving into accommodation for the first time, and it's easy to forget to do them when you are excited by your new surroundings and newfound independence.

The inventory isn't just to protect the landlord's property and fittings, but **it will also protect you from 'financially creative' landlords who may try to withhold your deposit at the end of the tenancy on the pretext of damages.** The inventory can save you hundreds of £s in damage recharges. They are essential and MUST be signed by the tenant. If they are not signed they cannot be used in a dispute.

The inventory is a listing of the items within the property and it helps with the assessment of damages during the rental period. There will therefore be check-in and check-out inventories carried out so that comparisons can be made.

The quality of inventories varies massively. Some landlords don't even complete them or simply complete a listing of the items. This is completely inadequate for you, because there are likely to be existing marks, scratches, chips, tears on furniture and fittings, or even missing light shades for which you should not be held responsible.

You cannot afford to trust a landlord simply because they seem honest. When money is involved, people change their attitude as fast as a shark changing direction 180 degrees! This is where the disorganised or profit-motivated landlords will try to withhold your deposit on the premise that it was you who damaged their property. This is also why it's so important for the inventory to be thorough and accurate. Remember, we could be talking about more than £1000 of your money.

Agents frequently complete the inventory themselves on behalf of the landlord or sub-contract it to an inventory clerk. They are still likely to be superficial because a comprehensive inventory takes a couple of hours to write up, and this becomes expensive. Agents and landlords are unlikely to pay for high quality service providers because their core business is built upon small margins.

As a landlord, I complete my own inventories. I list and photograph every bit of furniture and all the fittings, specifying the makes and models of equipment, e.g. the fridge and cooker. I also describe light fittings and wall colours and identify any items that are damaged. From experience, I've learned to make sure the camera automatically adds the date to images. This protects me and the tenant. The only possible dispute can be over what is deemed to be fair wear and tear. Now this may seem to you to be a bit over the top, but it's based on experience and it ultimately saves a lot of time and aggravation should there be a disagreement.

If it's possible to accompany the person completing the check-in inventory, I would recommend that you do this, as it will provide you with an opportunity to point out the flaws in the condition of any room or item, e.g. damaged paintwork or holes in the wall from the previous tenants. However, normally you are just provided with a copy of the inventory to check and confirm. Again, it's essential to check it, make changes and add comments where the condition is not as described.

It will cost you money if the inventory isn't accurate, so don't ignore it. You need to immediately check it carefully!

When you are provided with a copy of the inventory there is usually a time limit to dispute the accuracy of the content. There may be a clause in your tenancy agreement that states if no amendments are received within a seven day period of the date of the inventory then it is deemed correct, whether you have signed the document or not.

This is a fair clause because the longer it takes to return an inventory – from the landlord's point of view – the bigger the risk that any damages will in fact have been caused by the new tenant. Seven days is, to me, a reasonable amount of time for someone to check over everything. On the other hand, forty-eight hours is insufficient and if they want it returned during this period I suggest notifying the agent/landlord in writing if you can't complete it in time, e.g. if you were back at home for a long weekend.

If you don't agree with an item or description **make a note on the inventory.** This includes stains on the carpet or, for example, on the bottom of the curtains, chips on the kitchen work surface (these are important because water will be absorbed by the work surface and create a lot of damage over a period of time), on the bath, tiling/floor-covering and wall. Check for any wine stains on the carpet hidden by the sofa and damage to either the mattress or behind the headboard. Also specify the number of house keys received.

In order to protect yourself, **I strongly recommend photographing these flaws and attaching them in a typed document, preferably emailing them, as the quality of the picture will be greater than a printed copy, along with a PDF of your signed inventory so that you have a dated record.** It's hassle and time-consuming, but it can save you hundreds of pounds at the end of your tenancy.

As an alternative, you could take a video, but I suggest ensuring it's date-stamped and therefore indisputable. Video files are obviously large and not as easy to send over to your agent/landlord, but they can be a useful backstop of evidence should your landlord try to withhold your deposit. If you simply return the hard copy of the inventory don't forget to take a copy for your own file (and extra ones for each of your housemates).

If the landlord's inventory is substantially inaccurate then you could engage your own inventory clerk. They are likely to charge approximately £100 (depending on the property size and part of the country). If you do this ensure it's carried out as close as possible to the date of the landlord's inventory and, where possible, prior to your move-in day. You will also need to send a copy of the inventory to the agent and/or landlord.

If no inventory is supplied, I strongly recommend that you create your own, even if you don't wish to employ an inventory clerk.

 Send me an email if you would like a template.
im@smartstudentguides.com

IMPORTANT: You can be charged additional fees over and above your initial deposit for any losses or damage incurred during your tenancy, so retain a copy of the inventory for the check-out process so you can dispute any inaccuracies or recharges.

Other things to check and test:

→ **Note down the serial numbers of all the white goods.** These are also useful if you don't understand how an appliance works, as most manuals can now be downloaded from the manufacturer's website.

→ **Check that everything works properly.** If it doesn't then write it into the inventory and add it to your 'snagging,' i.e. faults list.

→ **Test all the sinks and the bath**, ensuring the taps are rigid, the plugs are present and that they hold the water so none of it drains away.

→ **Flush the toilets to ensure they not only flush, but refill correctly, and that when the cistern has been refilled** (the part that holds the water and is above the pan) it's quiet. If water continues to dribble into the pan, then the ball cock and refilling element needs adjusting or replacing. Apart from wasting water, the noise will also annoy you late at night.

Just another reminder…

Take meter readings for your electricity, gas and water and phone these through to your supplier. I would also suggest photographing these and retaining them until you leave, just in case there is a dispute.

It's your home

Clean! People's standards of hygiene vary considerably, so you will want to avoid potential infections. This is time-consuming, especially when the rooms look clean, but ask yourself if it's worth the risk of illness.

So, before using any utensils or kitchen equipment provided, give everything a thorough clean and wipe over with a disinfectant (read the label as some, e.g. Cillit Bang or bleach, are very strong and can adversely affect different materials), including the work surfaces.

In the bathroom, clean anything that can be touched, including the door handles and the door edges.

This isn't a nice thought, but you should also replace any bed linen and inspect the mattress for bed bugs (see the chapter on defects and infestations). You should certainly vacuum the bed on both sides, especially at the edges around the seams.

What to set up/consider when you've moved.

→ **Insurance**

It's likely that you will have a lot of technical, electronic and computing equipment, and maybe an expensive bicycle. Unfortunately, thieves know this so student areas are prime targets.

When you calculate the total cost of replacing all your belongings for insurance purposes, you will be surprised at their total value. Ask whether you can afford not to have insurance? Do also remember that you are living with a bunch of friends with whom you will be socialising. There are bound to be accidents and electronics plus liquids = destruction = high cost.

So, to keep your costs down, ask your parents to check their insurance policy, or contact their insurer directly to see if you are covered. If not, then do consider buying your own insurance cover and regularly backup all your files. These days it's very quick and easy. We no longer need scores of floppy disks! (If you've even heard of these!)

→ TV Licence

Unfortunately, students also need a TV licence, and they don't get a discount. This applies whether you live in halls of residence or a private house.

If you have a separate tenancy agreement for your room (i.e. you rent a room in a multiple occupancy house) you need a separate TV licence to watch or record TV in your room, even on a computer or laptop. If you live in a shared house (multiple people under one tenancy agreement) one licence may cover the whole property. Even if your non-university home address is licensed, you may still need a separate licence whilst you're living in student accommodation.

If the TV is supplied by the landlord, it is his responsibility to license it.

You can face a fine of up to £1000 if you don't have a licence, so check out how to pay at www.tvlicensing.co.uk

→ Post redirection

It's a good idea to arrange for your mail from your previous home address to be redirected via www.royalmail.com/personal/receiving-mail/redirection. The cost is approximately £40.00 for 12 months (prices vary depending on how long you choose to redirect for). You should also inform your university of your new address.

→ Emergency contacts

If you are lucky your landlord will have provided a list of emergency contacts. If not, ask for one. Failing that, it's a really good idea to have one pinned up in a communal area, preferably on a noticeboard. The

Students' Union will probably be able to supply one for you.

Rubbish collection and recylcling

In doing additional research for this book, I had a meeting with my local environmental health department who were very helpful and proactive due to the large student population in Bournemouth.

A couple of issues were highlighted that you need to know about.

→ **Bins**

✓ You will need a big wheelie bin for general waste and another one for recyclables, possibly two if the council only collects every fortnight. Your landlord should provide these and include them on the inventory. They are supplied at a cost by the council and should have a uniquely coded microchip so they are traceable (yes, people steal them).

✓ Your council may be able to visit and provide a survey for the amount of bins that you need. This is worthwhile because you don't want your refuse to be overflowing. Not only is it a health hazard, but your landlord could get fined and this will be passed on to you (currently the fine is approximately £80).

Ensure the bins are not only put out on the correct day, but are brought back in the same day after collection. Otherwise:

• Your bin could get stolen and you will have to pay for a replacement.

• If you put your bin out too early or leave it out too long the council could fine you for creating an obstruction. I'm not sure what 'too long' might be. Each council will have its own opinion. However, it's best to do it the same day, especially if you have upset a neighbour, because if you're prosecuted then it will show as a criminal record! At the time of writing, there's a fine of £60 per householder i.e. EACH of you (more if you fail to pay within 14 days).

→ **Cigarette butts**

Obvious and disrespectful littering is often noticed around student accommodation, as smoking indoors is usually not accepted.

The council in Bournemouth were offering cigarette pouches, so that partly-smoked cigarettes and dimps can be carried around discretely. So, if you smoke and want to be responsible about where you ditch your dimps, ask your council if they will provide them.

→ **Car parking**

Parking on pavements can be an issue. You obviously need to be neighbourly and not park right in front of your neighbours' houses. And you certainly don't want to obscure their driveway. However, I did get ticketed myself a couple of years ago while I was parked in front of an HMO as I looked over refurbishment work. There were double yellow lines on the road outside so I parked half in the driveway, leaving the other half of the car protruding onto the path.

I was ticketed within five minutes. The uncharacteristically human warden told me she had received complaints that pedestrians couldn't get past without walking into the road. Actually they could, but apparently the rule is that a double buggy needs to be able to pass on the pavement.

Bills

At the earliest opportunity, you should sit down with your housemates and agree how you will share money, rooms, bills, food and household items and chores.

 This needs organisation! To ensure all necessary bills are shared and paid fairly by everyone, **I strongly recommend that you set up a house bank account that everyone pays their agreed share into at the beginning of each term.**

This means that all your fixed (and most important) bills will be paid automatically. Any money left at the end of the term can be carried forward, used for socials or shared out.

Fixed bills

Bills such as the ones for the **TV licence** and **council tax** usually come as one lump sum and can be agreed and paid off immediately (or monthly) upon your arrival. (Also, don't forget your rent!)

As students, in most cases you won't have to pay council tax, but remember that you still need to let the council know your student status at the start of your tenancy. Be aware of the fact that if a resident in your accommodation is **not a student they are liable to pay council tax.**

Variable bills

You'll need to find out who the service providers are for your utility bills. As previously mentioned, ask your landlord or letting agent. Alternatively, provided there are no restrictions within your Tenancy Agreement, you can shop around using comparison websites, but you will need an idea of what the previous bills were.

Bills to check up on:

✓ Water and sewerage

✓ Gas

✓ Electricity

✓ Internet/broadband

✓ Landline telephone

✓ TV licence

✓ Satellite/cable TV or Entertainment packages like Netflix/Amazon Prime

As part of your rent, the landlord can pay the water bills, or they can be paid on a monthly basis depending on usage.

If your landlord pays all your utility bills, they should have a 'fair usage' clause inserted into your Agreement, so that they only pay for a specified amount of the utility bills, but anything above that figure is your responsibility.

Be aware that some landlords at the lower end of the market have been known to hide heating controls and even remove water-heated radiators, only providing an electric heater on a meter for each room. It complies with the law but it's mean and more expensive for the tenant.

It's not acceptable to withhold supplies of gas, electricity or water. If this happens to you, remind them that this is 'harassment' as defined under the Protection From Eviction Act 1977.

Payment of bills

For utilities, it's best to set up payments using a **Direct Debit (DD)** or a **Standing Order (SO).**

These are ways of setting up a regular payment to be made from your bank account (for example, on the first of each month or the first month of each quarter).

Invoices from suppliers will include a range of options listing how else you can make payments, so read the back of the invoice if you need to make a rapid payment by cash, credit card or bank transfer. Be aware that many suppliers (and banks) these days use premium rate, high cost phone lines that are understaffed ("we are exceptionally busy today...") and very slow to direct your call to an individual who can actually help. Draw your own conclusion on this commercial action...

Payment problems

If you don't pay your bills the suppliers will issue reminders. However, **late payment may show on your credit history** so you need to ensure that payments are made on time. Ultimately, if you don't pay, legal action (including the cost of a summons fee) may be taken, and the service could be terminated.

If you are having problems, I always recommend informing the supplier at an early opportunity. They are inevitably helpful and can put together a catch-up plan.

Another recommendation is to ensure that you check the meter readings, as suppliers will put forward an estimate rather than have someone visit to read the meter. Utility estimations and suggested payment plans are usually over-estimated so they would be charging you too much.

If this happens, I recommend you phone them with your own meter reading, or see if you can input your readings on their website. If a utility company makes a suggestion for how much you should pay each month as a payment plan, bear in mind that if you have been using gas and electric during the winter then your usages will be higher than in the following months. I always recommend underpaying than overpaying, so use this as an opportunity to negotiate. At the end of your tenancy it will all balance out and it's better having the money in your account than in that of a large corporate business.

Also, check the payments you make are correct and in line with your invoice. It has been known for duplicate payments to be made in error.

There is a lot to consider when you move in, so go through everything that I have suggested - especially the inventory section. Also, setting up a seperate bank account and talking through all of the bills associated with the house is SMART and will rule out unessesary arguments down the line.

CHAPTER ELEVEN

Living in Your Home

Figure 16 - Your ma deserves appreciation

Living in your new flat/room will be exciting, but unfortunately there are responsibilities that come with it; from bill paying (I'm sure you're getting an idea of that now) to general maintenance of your new place.

In the following chapter, I'll be sharing a few economical tips, plus the general maintenance you will be responsible for. Forewarned is forearmed, and having lived at home, you're probably not aware of some of the things I'll be mentioning, but ultimately it could be your responsibility to sort out (even if it's to get the landlord to fix it.)

Being Economical

How many students does it take to change a light bulb? Nobody knows because it's never been done...

You probably haven't had to concern yourself with living costs whilst you've been living back at home, with Mum and Dad insulating you from day-to-day living expenses. Real living costs may surprise you and certainly the amount of time it takes to keep a home in a nice condition is extraordinary. Hopefully, you will appreciate all the work that was done for you over the years, and maybe you will **send a loving thank you to your Ma and Pa.**

The average student debt when leaving university in 2015 was over £21,000 (in August 2016, I read how The Money Charity had stated that this year's new graduates will be suffering under the weight of a £41,000 debt due to an increase in tuition fees, a sum which would buy you a property in the north of England and many parts of Scotland – so if you would rather invest in property than a degree, then please get in touch!). When jobs are difficult to secure, it's sensible to contain your expenses and minimise the debt you will have to pay back. The Bank of Mum and Dad is not like the Bank of England; it cannot print money to repay debts.

I believe that you need to discuss budgeting issues with your parents before leaving home, as it's likely they'll be subsidising you. For this reason, budgeting has been missed out of this book, but if you think it should have been included then please email me.

However, because of my experience with refurbishing properties and enthusiasm to save money and improve homes, this chapter will help you reduce some of your 'operating' costs in the home and provide you with many practical solutions, which should make your abode more pleasant and easier to manage.

Before launching into this, I'd like to mention how student landlords have reported back that one of the biggest failures of students when renting is a lack of communication, i.e. not asking for advice or help. Sometimes this is about paying rent but frequently it is about problems in the property.

Maybe it's because they are unfamiliar with the problems, would rather not bother people or fear being charged an outrageous sum by an unethical plumber. What they fail to understand is that not fixing it can cause much bigger problems.

One example that happens often, I'm told, is to do with basins and baths not draining properly. Students cope with a slowly draining basin; it seems minor and as they can live with a small delay nobody in the house takes responsibility to get it fixed. That is until there is a complaint about the smell of the drains, or a leak all over the floor, or the room below complains water is leaking down the walls. Upon inspection, the cause is simply hair getting stuck in the waste pipe. It's easy to fix. I know from living with a family of three girls with long hair – I had to regularly unblock showers, baths and basins. For students, it's just a case of phoning the agent and telling them that the water isn't going down the plughole. They will get someone round to fix it. So don't be shy about phoning the agent and asking for help.

Having said that, if there's a spider in the bath you want removed, or the plastic pull on the bathroom light switch has fallen off, or you report a power cut but it's just a light bulb that has blown, or your kettle is faulty, well, these really aren't for the agent to attend to. By the way, these were actual requests made to agents I know.

The following are suggestions and ideas in domestic economics. Some may appear not to be worth the effort because individually they are not substantial. However, they require little effort and you will be amazed at how much you can save over a year.

How to save money

They are in no particular order, but here are some good tips:

→ **Central heating**

✓ Ensure it's **on a timer** so it's not on 24/7. *If you have an electric heater that doesn't have a timer then you can buy a plugin one from a DIY supermarket/warehouse or electrical wholesaler.* They are only a couple of £s but they will save you a lot of electricity. Ask the landlord if he will provide one.

Image 17 - Photo of a timer

✓ If your water is too hot to touch, then you are wasting a lot of electricity. Ask your landlord to **reduce the temperature on the thermostat on the hot water cylinder.** It's easy to do if you know what you are doing, but dangerous if you don't, so I won't describe it here.

✓ **Showering** only uses two-fifths of the amount of water that a bath consumes. It's not just the water that's saved, but the cost of heating it. When there are five of you living in a house, for instance, and there is only one bath, how long will it be before the water runs out? You need to give some thought as to how you can organise the use of the bathroom, otherwise the last two people will never have hot water.

It's okay to say you will put the immersion heater on to heat up some more water, but using one of these is expensive and can take a while to heat enough water for a bath.

If you have gas central heating, you obviously have a thermostat with which to adjust the overall temperature. However, if your own room is too hot you can adjust the temperature of the radiators by closing the valve. If the heat from the radiator varies at different positions on the radiator it needs attention. (See page 183)

→ **Electrical**

✓ **Dimmer switches** reduce the brightness of a light fitting, so they not only improve the range and quality of lighting moods, but they lower your electricity bills. I install these in bedrooms and lounges, so if you don't have them ask your landlord if they will do this. They are generally very quick to install (10 minutes) by someone who knows what they are doing.

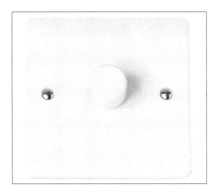

Image 18 - Photo of dimmer switch

✓ **Don't leave TVs or other electrical appliances plugged in on standby mode, as they continue to use electricity.** Simply switch off via the on/off button on the TV rather than via the remote control.

The same applies to phone and laptop chargers. With laptops, don't leave them plugged in charging all the time because the batteries degrade; they'll hold their charge for a shorter time which will become aggravating, and batteries are expensive to replace.

✓ **Put only as much water in the kettle as you need.** Putting more than this in will waste electricity and the quality of the water will reduce if you continually boil it.

The same applies to pans when you are cooking – don't over fill them.

✓ When leaving your accommodation for the holidays, it's a good idea to **turn the thermostat down and in the summer turn the central heating off.** It's even better if you have a timer that you can pre-set with the times the water and heating should come on.

✓ If there is a draught coming from around any of the external doors or windows, advise your landlord about it. If this is the case, you don't have a proper seal so the cold air is getting in, requiring additional heating. It's not difficult or expensive for the landlord to add a seal.

✓ **Light bulbs - choosing the right ones can save you money!**

LED light bulbs. I really like these and they use a lot less electricity. However, they are costly and are probably uneconomic for you to buy for a single year.

Energy saving light bulbs. These use a lot less electricity and they last longer. However, they are slow to reach full brightness, the quality of the light generated is cold and they frequently don't work with dimmer switches. They are a lot more expensive to buy and it's debatable whether they are actually environmentally friendly. You have probably guessed that I don't like them, but if you get 12 months regular usage then they may save you money. If it's for a light fitting that isn't used much, or there are only a couple of months left on your contract, or it's for your bedroom (where you should use a dimmer), I'd buy a standard light bulb.

In selecting your light bulbs, remember that the **higher the wattage, the bigger the power consumption.** This is another reason for having a dimmer switch. As an indicator, if you have a standard single pendant fitting in your bedroom, and it's a standard sized, e.g. 12x10 if you are lucky, then a 60w bulb should be adequate.

For a bedside lamp, 40w should be fine and in many cases 25w are suitable, except if you read a lot in bed. Be careful with lampshades because many of them have a maximum rating of 40w. This is because there is too much heat generated by bigger wattage bulbs and it's therefore a fire hazard. Read the label in the shade, as it will tell you the maximum wattage of bulb that should be used with it.

✓ **Don't leave fridge doors open and make sure they are shut**, not just pushed, because sometimes the door seal doesn't activate.

The same applies to freezers, but ice will build up over time. This will result in ice blocks forming in all the compartments, which will reduce your available space and make the freezer less efficient. It's time-consuming to defrost as well. So try to avoid the build up of ice.

Check the setting on your fridge. There is no point in over-chilling items. If there is a dial on your fridge marked one to six, for example, one is usually the lowest setting and six is the coldest. Anything over four is likely to freeze the contents. I never have the setting over three, and for many years in winter I've kept them at one point five.

✓ If you are lucky enough to have a washer-dryer, then be aware that the **dryer is particularly expensive to run**; it's much better if you can use a clothesline outside, as this also keeps condensation out of the house.

Failing that, try to dry them on a maiden near an open door or somewhere well ventilated. However, when there are a few of you, finding space to dry clothes and bedding is very difficult and you may have to use the dryer, especially in winter.

→ **Phone Calls**

Telephone numbers starting with 0845 and 0870 are classed as "non-geographic" numbers, which means they're not tied to a particular location. These numbers are usually used by large companies, banks, utility providers and public sector bodies.

Calls to 0845 and 0870 numbers may be free from your BT landline, depending on which plan you're on. This doesn't include dial-up internet calls to ISPs or calls to dial through or calling card access numbers. They can therefore be a lot more expensive to phone.

Calls to these numbers from your mobile will be expensive.

As previously mentioned, be aware that many banks, utility providers and government departments still use 0845 numbers so they get a refund from the high call charges.

 If you want to reduce the cost of your calls to these numbers, log onto www.saynoto0870.com and find the appropriate webpage and type in the 0845 number. The website will give you alternative landline phone numbers. You can also download an app for your mobile.

General Issues

Damp

This is one of the biggest problems for tenants and landlords. Unfortunately, it can be costly to remove, which can result in a tenant's deposit being withheld. So, for this reason, it's best to give some guidance on how to identify it, whose responsibility it is, and what you need to do.

Damp can cause mould on walls, furniture and clothes, and as mites feed on mould, it can increase the risk of respiratory illnesses in some people. It has a musty smell and also makes a room more difficult to get warm, so it isn't pleasant to live with.

Basically there are three types of damp:

1. Rising Damp

2. Leaks

3. Condensation

→ **Rising damp**

This is caused by the Damp Proof Course (DPC) of the house being damaged or missing, and as older houses were not built with a DPC, it's more likely to be found in these. It is noticeable, as you will see dark tidemarks on the wall, which will also feel cold. This will be on an exterior wall that is in contact with the ground (on rare occasions it can be found on an internal wall that divides rooms). Therefore you won't find it on a floor above ground level.

What happens is that over time the brickwork absorbs the water from the earth, which works its way up, resulting in damp marks on the wall. This is the landlord's responsibility, so you should inform them or the agent as soon as possible, otherwise the damp will spread.

Dampness will also result in a colder room, which will increase your heating bills.

If your landlord won't pay for the repairs (it can be expensive) then it's worth asking them to supply you with a dehumidifier, which will extract dampness from the air.

However, it's much better to spot this when you are doing your initial viewing and ask for it to be repaired before you agree to move in.

→ **Leaks**

If a brown patch appears on the ceiling or on the middle of a wall, or a wall not in contact with the ground, this will be a leaking pipe that will need immediate attention from a plumber. Do not delay taking action here as the problem may deteriorate rapidly. Water can be soaked up for months, and if it's a ceiling made of plasterboard it could just collapse through!

Frequently, the cause is a poor seal around a bath or a faulty plumbing joint. Have a look at the position of the stain and try to determine what is above it or which wall it is adjacent to. It may simply be from a dripping tap or showerhead and excess water is finding its way down the side of the bath, or from a wet bathroom floor (which could be caused by someone overflowing the bath when they get in it, a leak from the sink or the toilet), from where the water trickles into a corner and runs down. If you find this then at least you can prevent further damage. Call the landlord/agent who can arrange for a plumber to visit.

→ **Condensation**

When you are doing a viewing, you should be on the lookout for signs of damp, including that musty smell.

If it's there, it will return and you will probably get the blame for any required repairs or redecorating.

Condensation occurs mainly during cold weather, as cold air cannot hold as much moisture as warm air, so it deposits the droplets on cold surfaces. North facing walls are usually colder so attract more condensation. It also appears in places where there is little movement of air, such as windows and in or behind wardrobes and cupboards.

It will ultimately be your responsibility to minimise condensation. Breathing causes it, so its creation is unavoidable, but your lifestyle can make it considerably worse.

If you don't make an effort to minimise condensation, you will end up with mould forming on walls and fabrics, including your clothes, and it will result in your room requiring redecoration and professional cleaning, for which you are likely to be charged.

To minimise the amount of moisture in the air, the following actions are recommended:

✓ Put lids on saucepans whilst they are boiling (this will also mean you can lower the temperature of the hob).

✓ Switch the kettle off if it doesn't turn off automatically.

✓ When cooking, switch the kitchen extractor on (if one is fitted) or open a window.

✓ Open a window or switch on the extractor if you are having long showers or baths (this is SO important if your bathroom doesn't have a window, but many tenants switch the extractor off in order to reduce noise or to save a couple of minutes of electricity. This is a false economy).

✓ Do a final rinse when using the washing machine so there is less water to evaporate into the air whilst it's drying.

✓ Wipe down the windows and sills every morning when they are wet. Wring out the cloth rather than drying it on a radiator (which would evaporate the water back into the air again).

✓ Dry your clothes and bedding outside whenever possible, or put them on a maiden in the bathroom, but open a window or switch on the extractor and close the door. Drying clothes is one of the biggest causes of moisture.

✓ If you find mould forming on the walls or ceilings you need to quickly wipe them down.

Soapy water will do to start with and will improve the appearance of the wall, but you will need something stronger to kill it off. In the past I have used diluted bleach (using rubber gloves and being careful not to drip it, especially if there are fabrics nearby), leaving it on the surface overnight. However, it's better if you can wipe it down with a fungicidal wash, which carries a Health and Safety Executive approval number. As with all powerful chemicals, follow the manufacturer's instructions.

To remove moisture, you can ventilate your property without making draughts. Open a small window when it is comfortable to do so (during the night if you are warm enough) or leave a trickle ventilator open all the time if possible (these are the small lateral slats found above modern double glazing units).

In cold weather, the best way to keep rooms warm enough to avoid condensation is to use the thermostat on the central heating to keep a minimum temperature of, say, 18c.

Another tip that I haven't personally tried but am assured is very effective at removing excess moisture is to place half a bag of rock salt (it's cheap and easy to buy – just do an internet search) in a bowl in the corner of a room. This will draw moisture from the air, but you will have to empty it regularly and keep it topped up. It can also be used for keeping cupboards and wardrobes free from damp, although if you are finding damp here I suggest you neglected to do a proper inspection before you rented the property.

Defects

It's important that any defects within the accommodation are brought to the attention of the agent or landlord **as soon as possible**, so they can rectify the problem. If it's an issue that could cause an accident, e.g. a loose stair carpet, loose electrical wiring or a burst water pipe, then do this immediately.

Reporting defects

The landlord will want to get this fixed – they will not want an accident in their property nor the threat of being taken to court, even if they have public liability insurance. They also have a duty to respond to problems within a reasonable time. Having no heating or hot water, or a toilet that won't flush, are serious issues.

If the issue is serious, I'd expect the landlord or agent to respond within a few hours. The term "reasonable time" is intentionally vague because it is ultimately for a court to decide what is reasonable given the seriousness of the problem and the circumstances in trying to fix it.

> **My recommendation is to quickly phone then immediately back it up in writing.**

If no action is taken within your judgement of what is reasonable, I'd write to them again saying that unless they respond within 24-hours (less if it's a leak, for example), then you reserve the right to pay for the repair yourself and deduct it from next month's rent. If you have to get a tradesman in to carry out the repair, I'd also get two quotes for the work, so that the landlord cannot dispute the cost as you have tried to minimise their loss.

So, if you are too polite and you don't inform them of the problem, then the only person to blame is yourself.

Unwelcome guests/infestations

It is the landlord's responsibility to ensure that the property is free from any form of infestation.

As mentioned previously, a spider in the bath isn't an infestation...and neither is a floor full of pizza boxes. It isn't a hotel and you aren't yet successful enough to employ an entourage of minders and domestic staff. Unfortunately, litter is a regular problem with students. The boxes not only leave the room in an unsuitable state for studying, but they will become the rodent equivalent of a Starbucks, where friends meet for a bit of lunch...

Rodents

> **If you have rats in your property you must contact your local authority's environmental health department and ask them to get rid of them.**

Your local authority is less likely to deal with mice, but they will be able to give you advice. Ultimately this is likely to be something you will need to sort out with your landlord as part of their responsibility. However, before the landlord visits, ensure all the rooms are clean with no evidence of food lying around, otherwise the landlord may try to blame you for attracting rodents.

If the landlord calls in a company to eradicate an infestation, they will identify if bad housekeeping is the cause, and as a result are unlikely to guarantee their work. So, under these circumstances, if you have a re-infestation, you will probably incur a charge.

Bedbugs

According to the NHS, many people do not react to bedbug bites or only have an odd spot. However, although they aren't dangerous, they can be very itchy and unpleasant. They can also (apparently) crawl between rooms.

Here's some additional information so you know how to identify them and how to remove them.

How to spot them:

✓ Look for an unexplained skin rash or itchy bumps on your skin.

✓ Look out for black spots on your mattress – this could be their dried faeces.

✓ Look for mottled shells that bedbugs may have shed.

✓ Check your sheets for blood spots where you may have rolled over and squashed a bug after it had fed.

✓ Using a torch, inspect all the crevices and joints of your mattress and furniture to see if you can spot any bugs.

A landlord is supposed to respond quickly to a report of a bed bug infestation and start action within 24-hours. Ultimately, if a landlord fails to take action in an acceptable time frame, tenants can take action themselves. You can deduct any costs from your rental payments (immediately put in writing what you are planning to do, then confirm in writing when you have done it and how much you will be deducting).

To get rid of bed bugs, dust mites and other bugs:

✓ Take off the sheets and strip down the bed to the mattress.

✓ Spray your mattress, pillows and around the bed with specialist disinfectant chemical spray that can kill this type of bug (read the label first and follow the instructions carefully).

✓ Vacuum the bed and pillows. This may involve standing on the bed and using your vacuum like you do when you do the floors.

✓ Use fresh sheets and blankets with double pillowcases on the pillows.

You may need professional help for a particularly large or widespread infestation. The above may not work, as bedbugs are very small and difficult to remove, so it's wise to contact your agent or landlord and ask them to arrange for a pest controller to visit.

To save yourself from a possibly large deposit deduction, whatever the condition of your mattress, **invest in a fitted mattress protector.** Agents tell me that many landlords recharge for the cost of a new mattress because it's stained and new tenants have refused to rent a property as a result. So, no drinking coffee or beetroot Nutriblast in bed.

Mattress stain removers are also available, and you can search for them on sites such as Amazon.

General House Maintenance

It's not my place to encourage you to do any DIY, but there are a number of things that you should know that you probably weren't shown at home. They could save you a lot of money or inconvenience, and I'm sure there will be improvements that you will want to make that will make your property a more comfortable home.

Many things can be done without having to wait several days for your landlord or agent to explain something or arrange a repair.

A landlord I know had tenants who requested for the batteries in their Sky remote be replaced. Honestly! I think you can manage this without instructions.

Replacing fixtures

Indoors you can replace electrical fixtures such as bedside and desk lamps, just make sure you keep the ones that were there already so you can refit them when you leave. Be careful if you want to replace light fittings or switches (e.g. dimmer switches), as any wiring should be carried out by professionals and agreed with the landlord.

Moving furniture

Undoubtedly, you will want to make the accommodation as comfortable as you can to suit your lifestyle. This may sound patronising, but as tenants of all ages make these mistakes, I will mention them. First, be careful when moving furniture to ensure you don't drag the item and either snag the floor or damage the item's legs or scrape it along walls and/or bump into other items (especially curtains).

Be especially careful in the kitchen. Standalone fridges have an electric lead to a wall socket that may not be very long, and standalone cookers are likely to have a shorter lead, or, if they are gas, may be immovable. So be very careful as you could damage the gas supply pipe.

I have heard of numerous occasions where a fridge or freezer was reported as not working, but on inspection it was discovered one of the tenants had pulled the plug out in order to do the ironing or charge their phone and then not replaced it! D'oh!

If the plug for the fridge or freezer is in sight ask the landlord to paint it red or attach a coloured label to the wire (not the plug because paper near a plug is a fire hazard).

Decorating

I was going to write this section as a single word. The word was:

DON'T!

However, I had second thoughts because some things are not obvious.

You need to remember that the house isn't yours. Any changes can financially impact the value of the property or its ability to be rented. Your accommodation may need a coat of paint, but it's the landlord's decision, not yours. I refurbish properties, so I know that the standard of most people's DIY is atrocious. Redecorating isn't simply about putting another coat of paint on the top of the existing one.

In a rental property, you must get permission even to put up a picture or mirror. Before putting anything on the walls you must ask the landlord if it's okay and get this in writing, as it can be seen as damage for which you could be charged and end up in a dispute about.

Some will allow you to paint, provided that you restore the room(s) back to its original colour. If you aren't staying for very long it is a lot of effort and an unnecessary expense. If you are insistent, it may be worth discussing colour with the landlord, but a neutral palate is more acceptable and it's unlikely that the landlord will want you to paint it back to the original colour before you leave.

If there are colours, items or grubby paintwork you really dislike you can still ask your landlord if they would be prepared to change a couple of colours, or if they would be willing to replace a grotty floor covering, especially if it's a dirty, wet carpet in the bathroom. Again, it's best to do this when negotiating to rent the property, as this is when the landlord is most likely to want to help because he or she will need to secure the rental.

The tenants of one landlord I know decorated the bedroom walls black and the ceiling dark blue with silver stars on it. It was inappropriate for me to laugh when he told me this, as I should have expressed sympathy. Repainting over dark colours is a huge and labour-intensive task, so it's therefore costly. You don't want to be faced with such a recharge, especially as it will take time to repaint and may result in the property not being rentable. It could also result in you being recharged for the rental void period!

Crack in a light switch or socket

If you see one of these, then immediately inform your agent or landlord and ask them to get it replaced, as it could be dangerous.

Replacing light bulbs

Light bulbs blow and will need to be replaced. In a survey carried out in 2007, it was revealed that 25% of people under the age of 35 weren't sure how to change a light bulb. So, I reckon it would be remiss of me not to provide some guidance, even though in an HMO the responsibility for replacing light bulbs rests with the landlord.

There are a couple of different fitment types and fitting sizes. I will only cover the traditional bulb fittings for ceiling lights and bedside lamps. This will account for over 90% of all bulbs that will need replacing in an HMO.

Suffice to say, if there are problems then speak to your agents or landlord.

If a bulb blows, you'll need to switch off the light or lamp so that the connection is no longer live and you won't get an electric shock. Don't try to remove it for a couple of minutes, as it will be very hot. When handling bulbs, don't grip them too tightly or put them under pressure, as they are made from glass. It's unlikely, but not impossible, to shatter them.

The most familiar fitting in the UK is the bayonet fitting, which has two prongs that hold it in place in the lamp holder. You will find these in most ceiling lights where there is a single bulb in a shade that hangs from a pendant.

Figure 19 - Lightbulb - Bayonet fitting

To remove the bulb, you'll need to push it in gently to release the clamp then twist it anti-clockwise for a quarter of a turn. It will just loosen from the holder so you can pull it out.

The screw fitting was the standard European fitting and is now found in many homes. You simply unscrew the bulb until it becomes loose from the socket.

Figure 20 - Lightbulb - Screw thread, normal type

Figure 21 - Lightbulb - Screw thread, thin screw

Although the current in a light fitting is comparatively small, do not put your fingers inside the socket. Unlike in a cartoon, a selfie will not show your hair standing on end as a result of an electrical shock!

When you remove the old bulb, look at the top, as it should show the wattage. Each lampshade should also have a label that shows the maximum bulb wattage. This is because higher wattage bulbs generate more heat, so you must not exceed the level on the label, even if the previous bulb was of a higher wattage – it's not worth the risk of combustion.

I always check that it's the bulb that has blown because it may be a fault elsewhere in the fittings (other people's DIY can be less than reliable). So I use a bulb from another fitting that I know is working. If this bulb doesn't work then you need to quickly get in touch with your agent or landlord, as it's likely there is a loose wire and this is a job for an electrician. In this case, you don't really want to be touching the lamp holder or switch.

Assuming that it's just the bulb that needs replacing, simply insert it into the holder and screw in as appropriate. If it's a screw fitting, be aware that there are two thicknesses of screw thread so make sure that you have the correct style and don't over tighten it.

Turn the light back on to test that it works okay. Dispose of the old bulb.

Downlighters are now a lot more popular, as they fit flush into the ceiling. However, they can be a pain to replace as you ideally need a suction pad, but the bulbs sometimes break in their sockets. There are different voltage versions as well, so I won't describe how to take them out. As a landlord, I am not keen on tenants trying to replace them. However, if you have (more expensive) LED versions fitted then that's good news because they are cheap to run and are unlikely to need replacing during your tenancy.

Anyway, for purposes of recognition, *see figure 22* over the page for what it looks like.

Figure 22 - GU10 downlighter LED version.

Freezer

If the inside walls of your freezer get covered in ice it can be a major inconvenience. This is caused by the door being left open or, more specifically, not being fully closed. This can result in the doors refusing to open or push back in (with the added risk of damage), reducing the available space by half and using up a lot more electricity.

Defrosting is a lot of hassle to do once you have moved in and filled your freezer, so ideally you should have checked it on your initial viewing and had the landlord agree to defrost it before your moving in date.

If you've reached this stage and need to defrost your freezer, you need to be organised. Tell your housemates and run down the contents of the freezer to a minimum, preferably only leaving contents that can be refrozen.

Turn the freezer off at the wall socket and open the door. Remove the contents and leave the door open.

Now you can just let it defrost. If you do this you will need a couple of towels on the floor to mop up the melted ice. However, as it will take a few hours, your contents will defrost too, making a lot of it unusable.

As many items cannot be safely refrozen, read the labels first to check the freezing instructions.

Rather than leave your freezer defrosting overnight, if you want to speed up the process you can do this yourself in approximately an hour. As it's important not to let items defrost, get yourself a large cooler bag and transfer the freezer's contents into this. Then take out all the removable compartments/drawers, wash them out and leave them to dry. However, if they are frozen in, do not pull hard as this may damage them. Simply leave them in place until you can easily remove them. To melt the ice, place bowls of freshly boiled water on each shelf and keep the freezer door open. Mop up any melted ice with a towel and squeeze this out. You will need to repeat this a number of times. You can also use a freezer ice-scraper to GENTLY scrape away some of the ice. Do not use a chisel or knife or you may damage the inside of the freezer.

Once you have removed all the ice, clean the inside of the freezer and around the door seal with a clean towel. Remove any excess water before replacing the drawers and filling the freezer up again.

When Things go Wrong

Broadband not working

If your broadband stops working, the chances are that it's a technical problem with your computer, software, the supplier has a fault or the hardware/router is faulty. This is something you will need to get fixed quickly, but it's not something that the agent or landlord is usually responsible for. If you arranged for it to be installed then phone the supplier.

Electrical cut out

None of your electricity is working. This could be because:

a) **Your master switch on the consumer unit has blown/tripped out.** This may have been caused by some recently plugged in equipment that is faulty or has overloaded the circuit. If you have an instruction book for your consumer unit or your landlord explained how to reset the switch, then follow those instructions. Otherwise, phone your landlord or agent.

b) **There has been a power cut outside.** Telephone your supplier to advise them of this occurrence or to get an update on when it will be fixed. Before doing so, check to see if there are any lights on in the street or speak to your neighbours to see if they have the same problem.

c) **Your electricity is metered and you need to put more money in.** Don't laugh; other landlords tell me they've received calls from tenants complaining there is no electricity many times. D'oh!

Faulty electrical items

Many household appliances that consume a large amount of electricity have a master switch ('fused spur') that shuts off the electrical current to the appliance.

If an appliance isn't working, **then there is a very good chance it's caused by the master switch being off**. You will need to locate it, which is why it's best to ask where these things are when you are being shown around a property.

As an additional inconvenience, they aren't always located close to the appliance.

The main items that are likely to have a master switch are:

→ **Cooker/hob** – This is usually located on a wall close to the cooker, with the switch socket being much larger than the others and having a red switch.

→ **Oven** – If it's separate to the hob it's likely that the connection is via a plug socket inside an adjacent cupboard, or on the back wall adjacent to the hob.

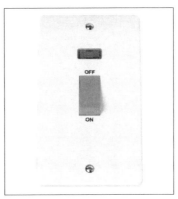

Figure 23 - Cooker switch

→ **Kitchen extractor** – This is usually located inside an adjacent cupboard, although I did once find one on the top of a kitchen cupboard where it was out of sight.

→ **Bathroom extractor** – This is usually located outside the bathroom high up on the wall near the door, or on a pull switch inside the bathroom.

→ **Electric shower** – The master switch is usually located in an airing cupboard inside or adjacent to the bathroom, although I have had flats with a second pull switch. If it's for a recently refurbished en-suite it's likely to be on the wall in the bedroom near to or above the door leading to it.

→ **Washing machine or dishwasher** – This can be located on a wall close to the appliance or, more frequently, inside an adjacent cupboard where there will be an electrical socket with a plug from the appliance.

→ **Electric radiators** – These will be plugged or wired-in close to the radiator.

Other failures

Light doesn't work

This is probably caused by a bulb blowing, so just replace with a bulb that you know is working.

Oven or hob not working

A frequent cause of an oven not working can be that the **timer needs setting first**, so find your instruction book and read how to set it. Alternatively, look on the oven for the make and model number and search for instructions on the internet.

If it's a gas hob and if there is no smell of gas, then it's likely that the main gas switch needs putting into the on position. If there is a smell of gas and it's not igniting, then it could be that cleaning fluids have blocked the ignition. If you've had the gas on for some time, open the windows and let it dissipate. It's dangerous so it's best not to try to light it at this stage. Call your agent or landlord.

Item fallen behind the kitchen cupboard

Sometimes floor-standing kitchen cupboards have had the back panel removed or partly cut out. This is usually to access pipework or meters. Unfortunately, you can inadvertently push an item through so it drops off the shelf and you can't reach it.

However, you can retrieve the item by removing the kickboard panel that sits on the floor, underneath the cupboards. If it's urgent, get your agent or landlord to remove the kickboard so you can get underneath. You are likely to need a torch, but be careful as there can be all sorts of detritus underneath (usually untidy builders who have left nails and sawdust or food), so wear gloves

A valuable item has fallen down the sink or bath

It happens, but don't despair, because more than likely it will have simply dropped into the trap or u-bend underneath the sink or bath.

If you know what you are doing, it's not difficult to remove kitchen sink or bathroom basin wastes, and it can be done in 10 minutes. However, if you are unsure then don't try it because you will end up with broken connections or a serious leak! Baths are more complicated as the bath panel can be difficult to remove and reposition and the trap hard to reach. Hopefully your agent or landlord can do this for you as a favour, but make sure they give you a quote if they say a plumber will be needed.

Figure 24 - Bottle trap usually found under a bathroom basin

Figure 25 - U-bend with two adjustable 'arms' which are usually found under kitchen sinks, with the 'arms' being connected to pipes for a washing machine or dishwasher.

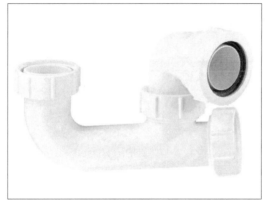

Figure 26 - A typical bath trap. This style is frequently used, as there isn't much space underneath a bath.

Dripping tap

If one of your taps is dripping it can be rather annoying, and over time it will waste quite a lot of water. The longer it is left without being fixed the worse the leak will become.

Obviously, the first thing to do is tighten the tap a fraction more (finger tight only). Don't over tighten by using all your strength because it will ruin the washer and probably increase the amount of dripping, and it may make the tap very difficult to open. The washer will probably need replacing.

If finger tightening the tap doesn't work, then contact your agent or landlord as quickly as possible. **This is normal wear and tear, so don't let them try to charge you.**

Smelly drains

This is an unpleasant smell emanating from your sink or hose connection to your washing machine. It's simply a build-up of kitchen grease, food detritus and detergents in the pipework.

Check for these smells before you move in. If they are present add them to your list of items that need fixing by the agent/landlord before you move in, otherwise you will get blamed for it.

At this point, I should remind you that sinks are NOT waste disposal units. Neither are dishwashers (if you are lucky enough to have one). Do not squash food down the plughole because it's likely to get trapped in the pipework and block the drains.

For your own sake, scrape as much food as you can directly into your bin before doing the washing up.

So, if the drains start smelling some time after you have moved in, you will need to clean them. Just buy a drain cleaner from the local supermarket and follow the instructions. It should dissolve the grease and gunk.

You'd be surprised by the amount of hair that gets trapped in bathroom plugholes, which grease and detergents attach to, so you should regularly pull this up from the basin before it drops through and causes a blockage. Ladies, your long hair is usually the culprit, so if you can't pull it out with fingers use a pair of tweezers.

Subsequent to writing this book, I have been informed by a well-respected landlady that there is another, easy way to unblock sinks, which I think will appeal to students. Now, I haven't tried this myself, so I take no responsibility for it, but it's worth giving it a go. Apparently, if you pour a two-litre bottle of cola (any brand, but not sugar-free) down the plughole and leave it for 24-hours, it will clear most things. However, you MUST wipe the cola from around any chrome or metal surfaces immediately to avoid damage, as the 'cleaning agent' in cola is phosphoric acid. You should also rinse the plughole with hot water.

Apparently, it's also very effective at cleaning toilet bowls. Email me if you have any success with this.

No hot water

If there is a mixer tap, i.e. both hot and cold water run through a single spout, then turn the lever fully in both directions. Let them run for a couple of minutes because in old houses especially, the hot water can have a long way to travel before it reaches the tap. The hot should appear from the left side and cold on the right. However, sometimes they are plumbed the other way around!

If there is no hot water reaching the bath or sinks then it's likely that the hot water cylinder or boiler isn't doing its job. This is most likely to be located in an upstairs cupboard, so check that the timer is working and that the master switch is on. You need to ensure the timer is on for at least an hour before you wake. To see if the water can be heated, find the immersion heater switch and turn it on. You should hear the water in the cylinder start to bubble as it heats up. If not, just leave it heating for half an hour then test the water to see if it's getting hotter.

If you don't have a cylinder, then it's likely you have a newer and different type of boiler (probably a combi boiler) that heats the water before pumping it around the house. Again, check that the master switch is on and the timer is set as you need it.

With a combi there is another possibility, and that is that there is insufficient pressure. On the front of the boiler is a gauge. If it registers 0 then it's likely that this is the cause of the problem, so contact your agent or landlord and ask them to get this fixed.

If it's an electric shower it may be that the electric master switch is turned off, which means that the water isn't heating up. There is usually a red light on the switch to let you know when it is on.

If it's a shower that gets heated up by the boiler, just test to see if there is hot water running in the bath.

No heating

First of all, if you have a pre-paid card meter check the card is inserted fully, and make sure that there is credit on the account (when you first move in there may not be). **At this point, I will also say that pre-paid meters are a lot of hassle, as you will continually have to go to the shops for top-ups (assuming there is a local reseller), as well as the fact that the utilities are more expensive to use than in normal meters. I would certainly ask the landlord to replace these meters before moving in.**

Cold or partially warm radiator

If the heating is on and other radiators are working, there are a couple of things that you need to check.

If the radiator is cold all over, it's likely that one of the valves is switched off. There is an input and output to a radiator, and if you are lucky you will have what is called a TRV valve, a Thermostatic Radiator Valve, on one side. Turn this anti-clockwise to open it up so that the highest number is in line with the indicator line/arrow. (*See figure 7* on page 59)

If it's an older-style valve, again, just turn it anti-clockwise to open it up to the maximum. See if that works. If the central heating is on you should feel the heat from the water reaching the lower part of the radiator and in the supply pipe underneath it.

Now, you need to make sure that the whole of the radiator heats up, so give it 10-minutes or so. If the radiator doesn't heat up at the top after half an hour or so, but the lower part is hot, then it's likely that your radiator has air in it.

To expel the air you need a radiator key and a cloth to catch the drips or spray if you open it too far.

Radiator keys are inexpensive to buy so you can get them at any DIY merchants or building/plumbing trade suppliers. However, ask your agent or landlord to do it first.

Figure 27 - Photo of radiator bleed key

Figure 28 - Photo of radiator bleed valve

At the top of the radiator on one side there will be a nut that the key fits over. Place the key over it and keep a cloth around it, not just to collect water that may leak but also to protect your hand, as the water may be very hot. Slowly turn the nut half a turn and you should hear the radiator hissing as air escapes.

Keep checking the radiator, as you should feel the heat rising up it as the air is pushed out. Eventually the valve will start coughing water out. At this stage, close the valve and leave for several minutes, then repeat the process to force out any remaining air, as this will collect here at the highest point.

If the radiator is hot at the top and cold at the bottom, it's probably due to a collection of sludge in the radiator. This happens over time and it is not your fault.

This is not a simple DIY job and will probably mean the whole heating system needs flushing out (preferably with your radiator being removed and flushed separately), so get in touch with your agent or landlord.

It isn't acceptable to have no hot water or an inadequately heated room. The landlord needs to attend to this within 24-hours, and don't let them try to blame or charge you for the work.

If the landlord doesn't spring into action, then advise them in writing/email that you will be getting it repaired and deducting the cost from your rental payment. After it has been fixed make sure you get an invoice then write or email again confirming the repairs and the amount that you will be deducting.

Blocked drain

To avoid the drains blocking up, don't pour cooking/meat fats down the sink because when they cool they will solidify. This can be expensive to fix and will also cause unpleasant odours. Let the fats cool and congeal before scraping them into the bin. If they are oils, pour them into a small bag that can be sealed or tied.

See the earlier comments about using cola, as this could unblock your sink or basin.

Paper towels or hand wipes can block the toilet because unlike loo paper, they don't disintegrate when wet. Best to have a small bin in the bathroom.

Apparently, if sanitary products etc. have blocked your toilet you can pour down a large cup of fabric conditioner, leave it overnight and follow that with a bottle of cola and it will clear it. As previously mentioned, don't leave chemicals or coke on metal. It's important to wipe them off immediately.

Water leak

If there is water leaking (a lot more than dripping) or spraying onto your floor, especially in your bathroom and kitchen, and you realise you need a plumber, you need to prevent water reaching the leak. You don't want a flood or water draining down into the floor below.

If it's a serious leak then the best thing to do is switch off the mains via the stopcock (turn the valve clockwise). This will stop your system from refilling from the mains.

It's therefore important that you know where the stopcock is. You will find it where the water supply enters the house. This is usually under the sink in the kitchen, or in a cupboard in the hallway. Or, if it's a single-storey building, it's usually in the bathroom. In a flat it can be in a cupboard in the hallway outside. You should be shown where this is when you move in.

Figure 29 - Photo of stopcock. In this case there are two because they are for adjacent flats. The wires are 'earthing straps' for the electrics.

However, switching off the mains won't stop water draining out of the tank (should you have an older system), which is a very large container usually located in the loft in a house or in a cupboard near the bathroom in a flat. So, you need to isolate this. If it's in the loft I suggest that rather than climbing up into what is usually a dark and dirty area, you should look for isolators that will be located near to where the leak is occurring.

If the leak is from the bath or one of the sinks then there may be an isolating valve in the supply pipe underneath the tap, or just underneath the toilet. This needs a screwdriver to turn the valve 90 degrees in order to close it (the slot for the flat-headed screwdriver needs to be at 90 degrees to the direction of the flow of the water). Getting at the bath may be a problem, as you will need to remove the access panel or the whole of the bath panel. Sometimes it's not apparent how to remove these, and they can be screwed and siliconed in place.

Figure 30 - Photo of isolating valve. One is for hot and the other is for cold water supplies to a kitchen tap.

Alternatively, if the leak is from the washing machine or dishwasher (if you are lucky enough to have one), then there are separate valves located near to the appliance where the hoses are attached to the pipework. These can be turned 90 degrees with your fingers to close them (don't force it). The levers are plastic and usually blue for the cold supply and red if there is a hot supply.

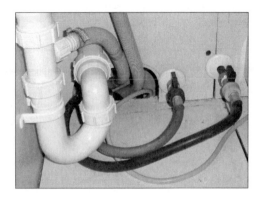

Figure 31 - Photo of washing machine valves

Now ring the landlord or managing agent and tell them what has happened. Ask when it will be fixed as it should be a top priority. It's not acceptable for this to be any longer than 24-hours.

Toilet dribble

Toilet cisterns fail. I even had two new ones that needed replacing within 12 months of installation. What happens is that after you have flushed, the cistern refills but water continues to trickle into the pan. This obviously wastes water (this will cost you money if you have a metered system). It also continues to make a noise, which can be irritating if you are trying to sleep.

If water continues to dribble into the pan, then the ball cock or refilling element needs adjusting or replacing, so inform your landlord straight away. This is wear and tear and so it's not your responsibility to pay for it.

Low pressure in shower

If there is only a trickle coming out of the showerhead, first check that the hose isn't leaking, as this will drop the pressure. Then have a look at the showerhead itself. You may find there is a build-up of lime scale that is preventing water from coming out of the spray holes.

A quick clean with a nailbrush or an old toothbrush should clear most of this. Retest it, but if there is still very little water spraying out then get in touch with the agent or landlord.

It isn't acceptable to have a shower that's just a dribble.

Stains

There are such a wide variety of stains and fabrics that the subject requires specialist advice. So, the only general advice I can give is to treat the stain quickly, and keep handy absorbent cloths and an old towel. You don't want the stain to set as that can end up taking a lot more time to remove, or worse, it can't be removed. This damage will cost you when you vacate the property.

Get on the internet straight away and type in "stain removal". There are expert websites that explain what you need to do for all different types of spillages and stains. Even better, get a book on it so you have a handy reference just in case your internet connection is down.

Also, be aware that Blu Tack leaves grease marks on paint, so try not to stick things up on a wall that is painted with emulsion. It's always a good idea to ask the agent or landlord what colour and manufacturer was used for the decoration, so you can touch-up where necessary. Also ask if they have an old can of the paint that can be stored at the property.

Vacuum cleaner stops working

If there is no power and the motor isn't spinning, check that the plug wasn't pulled from the socket when the cleaner was being pulled around the room.

If that doesn't solve it, try plugging it into another socket.

If that fails too, unplug the cleaner and check the power cord, as it may be that you have run over it and damaged it, or caused a short circuit.

If that's the case do not plug it back in as it will be dangerous. You'll need to get a new cord fitted.

Also be aware that some cleaners cut out when the collection bag is full, and others get temperamental when they are used on thick rugs, or, for example, when they have been set for use on a wooden floor and you are cleaning a rug.

If emptying the collection bag still hasn't solved the problem, check the fuse board or consumer unit to see if a fuse or circuit has broken.

Vacuum cleaner doesn't pick up crumbs

The chances are your vacuum cleaner isn't picking up crumbs because the collection bag is full.

If it's not this then you need to put the cleaner on its side and switch it on to see if the roller is working. It may have stopped spinning or it may be clogged with hair and carpet pile. If it looks clogged then switch the machine off and try to remove the offending item.

Vacuum cleaner smells of burning rubber

The likelihood is that the smell of burning rubber is being caused by the fan belt snagging or burning out. Fortunately, they are easy and cheap to replace if you know what you are doing.

If you are going to take a look yourself, make sure that the cleaner is unplugged from the electricity.

Vacuum cleaners are all different, so I won't describe what to do. If it's the landlord's then ask him or her to repair it. If it's yours then look for a small local electrical shop that will do this for you. It's worth getting them to service the cleaner at the same time, as they are likely to have filters that need replacing. This is something that most people neglect or aren't aware of and this is one of the reasons why so many vacuum cleaners are dumped at recycling centres.

If you are going to buy a vacuum cleaner, I suggest getting a Henry.

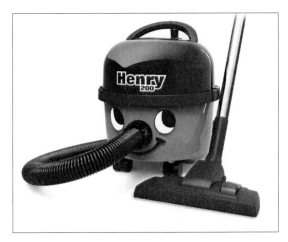

Figure 32 - Photo of a "Henry" vacuum cleaner.

Although these vacuum cleaners aren't fashionable, many commercial cleaners (and many tradesmen) use them. They are inexpensive (half the price of most cleaners), easy to drag around and unlike most domestic vacuum cleaners, they don't have a number of hidden or expensive filters to replace, or rollers to get snagged. They are minimum maintenance, which is what you need.

That's covered day-to-day maintenance, so now I will move on to some other important issues.

Gardening and Outside Maintenance

Some landlords may help with the maintenance of the garden, but this should be specified within your rental agreement.

Legally landlords don't have to provide you with a lawnmower, but some may be willing to help out, so it's always worth asking.

Gardening is a chore to most of us. If you have no inclination or time to do it, and the tenancy agreement states that it's your responsibility, ask the agent or landlord if they have a contact so you can get a quote for doing the work.

It may also be worth asking the neighbours if they have a contact, or if you could borrow their mower for a small fee.

In a shared property, it may be worthwhile sharing the cost of employing a contractor to cut the grass during the growing season.

Your responsibilities in the garden

As a tenant, it's your responsibility to keep the garden tidy, unless the landlord specifies in the agreement how the garden will be maintained. However, they should provide you with the hardware/tools to do this, but be aware that it's not a legal requirement.

You should also ensure that garden rubbish/lawn cuttings are disposed of.

Trees and hedges: you must not damage or cut down any tree in your garden unless you have permission to do so. If one is bothering you, let your landlord or agent know. The property may have covenants which state that certain types of trees have to remain or be replaced by similar ones (I've lived in a house where this was the case). In many areas, there are Tree Preservation Orders (TPOs), which can even restrict or prevent you from pruning trees let alone cutting them down. The fines for removing them can be enormous. A developer in Poole, Dorset (which is a notorious area for TPOs) was fined £20,000 for doing this!

Make sure that any approval is put in writing and dated.

Bonfires

As long as there isn't a clause in the AST preventing bonfires you are free to have one as long as you don't cause a nuisance with the smoke and smell and don't cause any risk to the property, other buildings or parts of a property, e.g. fences. It is also sensible and courteous to let your neighbours know in advance, just in case they had planned to be in the garden or to put their washing out.

I suggest that prior to having any bonfires you check the internet for any guidelines or laws from your local fire brigade, especially relating to the distance from the property and your legal position regarding damage and nuisance.

A couple of years ago, I helped a friend to do the gardening at a family property he had rented out, and we had a bonfire to burn all the prunings. Damaged fence panels also had to be disposed of. The bonfire was lit in an afternoon during the middle of the week when the neighbours were at work. All was well until the fire brigade unexpectedly turned up. Apparently, a passer-by wasn't expecting to see smoke so had phoned them in case there was a problem. I had cleared an area around the bonfire and even soaked the grass with water and had a hosepipe nearby (as a protection to prevent the embers from spreading the fire overnight).

Obviously, this had wasted the firemen's time, which is regrettable. I was told in future to ring the fire brigade before starting a bonfire to inform them of my plans. I am passing this message on to you, as it seems like a sensible thing to do.

Additional Structures

You must get written permission before you put up any additional structures, even sheds and aerials. This especially applies to satellite dishes, as there can be covenants on the property prohibiting or restricting their location. It's likely that if no houses on your road have a dish there will be a cable supplier.

So, it's important to ensure you have a satellite or cable connection before you move in.

Security – Being SAFE

This section is really important - please read carefully

There is more information about personal safety when out and about in Appendix 2 at the back of the book.

Students own more expensive consumer items per person than the average member of the population, so for thieves they are a lucrative and often easier target.

The most important part of security is your own common sense, because most thieves are impulsive. They are looking for easy pickings. Ensure all external doors and windows are locked when you are out and that all communal windows are closed at night.

If there are any fire doors in your property that are self-closing, do NOT wedge them open. It will put you at risk and will also invalidate any insurance.

Your housemates need to understand and action these as well.

Break-ins

If the house is broken into, the landlord cannot be held responsible and will not be liable. This is why contents insurance is essential.

The only circumstance where your landlord can be liable is if you made them aware of a broken door or window that was accessed during the break-in, but they hadn't made any effort to rectify the situation.

To make things easier for yourself in the event of a break-in, it's wise to do the following:

✓ Make a note of the serial numbers of all your hardware.

✓ Use invisible ultraviolet pens and write your name and address on all your belongings. This will make their recovery more likely.

✓ Mark items with a permanent marker pen, including the labels on your laundry, so that your personal items don't get mixed up with those of a less tidy housemate.

✓ Tell your landlord and neighbours when you are all on holiday or have gone back home, and ask if they can keep an eye on the property (don't forget to give them a present for doing this).

✓ Remove or hide all expensive electrical items. If you have a large TV, computer equipment or smartphone then put them out of sight, preferably in a locked cupboard.

✓ If you are on the ground floor, ensure people can't look into your room and see any valuables. Putting up net curtains is wise so casual passers-by can't see inside.

✓ Infrared lights for the back garden that come on at night will act as a deterrent, and these are especially advisable when there is an access gate or low fence.

In terms of the appearance of the property, you don't want to advertise that it's a student rental, otherwise it could become a magnet for ne'er-do-wells.

Here's some of the ways you could be unwittingly giving its identity away:

a) Posters or signs on the front door or in the windows (these may also be in breach of your tenancy agreement), or road signs and bollards that are seemingly self-propelled and have miraculously found their way into your garden.

b) Beer bottles, pizza boxes, over-full bins, etc., outside the property.

c) A downstairs front or back room that is visibly a bedroom.

d) Letting boards outside the property. Ask your agent to remove them. They are effectively advertising that students are present.

Agents will try to leave them up as free advertising (and some put them up even when there is no property to rent), so send them reminders. Personally, I pull them out of the ground, but if, for instance, they are attached to a wall you need to be careful not to damage the brickwork or mortar.

Student accommodation security checklist

✓ Do the front and rear doors have five-lever mortice locks (Kitemarked and stating five-lever on the visible plate) in addition to a Yale type lock?

✓ Is your house on the end of a terrace? These properties are more vulnerable than those in the middle, so you may need extra security.

✓ Does your house have a lane/alley at the rear? Does the property have a 'dusk 'til dawn' sensor light or prickly, hostile shrubbery that would deter a burglar? Houses that have lane access are much more vulnerable to a burglary.

✓ Does the property have patio doors? If so, do the locks work at the top and bottom?

✓ Is the front door visible from the street? Front doors blocked by shrubs or fencing make it easier for burglars to force entry into a property without being seen.

✓ As stated in an earlier section, if there is a ladder, make sure it can be locked away. If not, it's a major security risk, so request that either a lockable bracket is installed or the ladder is removed.

Fire

Fire is something that most of us don't really worry about. **We assume it won't happen to us, especially when we don't know of anybody who has experienced it.** Lots of tenants remove batteries from their smoke alarms because they are a regular irritation, sounding off and deafening us just because we are frying bacon. But by doing this you are putting your lives at risk, especially where there are groups of inexperienced people living together. When this is the case the risk of fire is much greater.

You may well have a fire extinguisher and a fire blanket, but if there is a serious blaze, the fire brigade say that your priority is to GET OUT and not waste time and risk your lives by trying to control it (which is why there should not be a fire extinguisher in an HMO).

Visitors

Each of you will probably have friends come to stay.

If you plan to have friends visit, as a courtesy ensure that your housemates are happy about this, especially if the intention is for your guests to crash out in a communal room. Obviously if it's for more than one night, then your guests will become more of an inconvenience, so please consider your housemates.

Notably, if you are in a relationship and want your guest to stay longer (and your housemates are happy with this) you need to be aware that…

✓ **If the property is occupied by more than the permitted number of people you could well be in breach of your tenancy agreement**, or even be in serious breach of the landlord's insurance or mortgage.

✓ **It might also mean that the house needs to be registered as an HMO,** so you need to ensure your landlord or letting agent agrees to it.

✓ **You also need to remember that any damage to the accommodation caused by your friends is your responsibility,** and that food and household bills will also increase, so be fair to your housemates.

Your privacy

The landlord or people acting on his/her behalf cannot enter at any time they choose in order to check the property or make repairs. This is called the tenants' 'right of quiet enjoyment'. However, this only applies if you **do not breach the tenancy agreement.**

> **The landlord must give 24-hours' notice to view the accommodation or do an inspection, although you may agree to less notice or request for the visit to be at a convenient time. If you then refuse entry you have no right to complain about any damage.**

If you are all out at the scheduled time and the landlord wants to continue with his inspection, **he must be accompanied by a witness**.

Being Conscientious with Your Neighbours

Moving into private accommodation is very different to living in halls. You need to become part of a community and respect others' lifestyles and privacy. Being seen or heard can be an unwelcome interruption to your neighbours' privacy and family life.

They may well have had students living next door to them last year, but that's not the issue. You don't want unhappy neighbours. Always consider the role reversal; what would your parents think or how would they react if they had students next door behaving like you are doing? What would the effect be if they were trying to sell that house?

So for your neighbours' sake and to avoid conflict, think about how they will feel if there are several people talking loudly, or in the garden, or banging doors or blaring music (that they probably dislike) out of open windows. Their annoyance will magnify if they commute and have to get up at 6:30am, and it will further increase if they have young children. They do not want to hear you, so be as polite and considerate as you possibly can.

A good start would be to make a point of popping round to your neighbours on the day you move in to introduce yourselves.

This will probably score you a lot of bonus points and help to create a friendly relationship. It will also mean they will be more likely to look after you, e.g. security, keeping a spare key and telling you about any water leaks. Why not give them your phone numbers so they can quickly get in touch with you, or ask if they need help with any heavy lifting, etc?

For their sake, and actually for your own security, refrain from advertising any parties, especially on Facebook or other social media.

Urban myth

Many students seem to believe that you have to cut out making noise after 11:00pm. This isn't correct, as the time varies in accordance with local council or property rules. There can be clauses that state, for example, no playing of musical instruments between 11pm and 7am. If you are making an unacceptable amount of noise then the time you are making it is irrelevant.

Some students will justify their behaviour by saying they invited the neighbours to the party, or they gave them a few cans of beer. Others maintain they gave them a week's notice or argue, "It's the only party we've had all year." So, did your neighbours agree in writing that you could have all the windows open with rave music blasting out at 140 decibels and the foundations vibrating from the bass and 50 people shouting in the garden and lobbing beer cans and cigarette butts onto the neighbours' lawns until 4am? Noise annoys.

There is no 'three strikes and you are out' rule. Statutory noise is defined as, 'A breach of quiet enjoyment of your property.'

Taxis

If you or any friends have to use taxis late at night or early in the morning (whatever happened to poor students who had to walk everywhere?), be aware that the rattling of a diesel engine whilst the driver waits for someone to get into the taxi and then the banging of doors and the sound of wheelie cases being dragged over the driveway is also disturbing for the neighbours. It's much better to have the taxi pick you up at the end of the road.

ABCs

The police can issue ABCs – Acceptable Behaviour Contracts, which are a preliminary to an ASBO.

CHAPTER TWELVE

Early Departure

Figure 33 - Off you go!

It's quite possible that you or one of your housemates will decide they have had enough and go back home. This is sad. Maybe it's down to a lack of persistence and confidence and it's been a waste of time and energy, or maybe it's a good, positive decision. I certainly regret not making a decision regarding the course of my career earlier, so I won't criticise someone who KNOWS the course is not right for them.

Maybe they have a great job offer or are entrepreneurial and are setting up a business. In which case, I wish them every success.

Anyway, if any of you decide to leave, you need to be fair to each other because if you rented together then you have an obligation to fulfil your contractual and moral obligations and pay a share of the bills until the end of the tenancy agreement.

However, a better solution would be to find another person who can move in. If you do this, don't forget to have the tenancy agreement modified. It may cost a few quid, but the person departing should pay and it's certainly worth it.

If you all decide to leave before the end of the term without giving notice and without the agent or landlord agreeing to it, this is known as "abandonment". It's important to understand that you still have to pay the rent until the end of the tenancy agreement and that the landlord can apply for a court order to make you hand over what you owe. Once you have a court order or rent arrears then you will find it more difficult to rent another property.

On the other hand, you may be involved with another form of early departure...the eviction. This can be justified, e.g. non-payment of rent, or a surprise. Either way, there is a legal process that the landlord has to follow. Let's get a grip...

Eviction

If your landlord threatens you with eviction, you should understand the grounds upon which this threat is being made. As timing is important, do not delay and **seek advice immediately**.

Before speaking with a solicitor, you should have a chat with the Students' Union, as it will be familiar with these issues and can point you in the right direction. Failing that, speak with the Citizens Advice Bureau or Shelter.

There are a number of legal issues involved, depending on the circumstances and the type of contract you have. It is an area that is too complex to explain or to give advice on, so I will just give you a broad outline.

> **Your landlord must follow strict procedures if they want you to leave their property, but if they don't follow these they may be guilty of illegally evicting or harassing you.**

It is illegal for landlords to evict tenants by using methods such as changing locks, physically throwing them out or preventing them from accessing either part of or the entire home. Should any of this happen to you then call the police.

Grounds for eviction

It would be unusual for a landlord to want to remove a tenant, especially part of the way through an academic year when there may not be many students who could take over the tenancy. Recently, there have been stories in the media about 'revenge' or 'retaliatory evictions' and new legislation has even been introduced. What a waste of parliamentary time. Landlords do NOT want to evict tenants who are paying full rent on time every month, look after the property and don't cause problems with the neighbours and council. Finding another tenant is costly and time-consuming.

Anyway, as a result, the Retaliatory Eviction and the Deregulation Act 2015 means that a Section 21 notice cannot be served within six months of a tenant making a genuine complaint about the condition of their property.

→ **During the fixed term**

During the fixed term of an AST, your landlord can only evict you for certain reasons. Here are some examples:

✓ You haven't paid the rent.

✓ You have been involved in antisocial behaviour. (See below)

✓ There's a 'break clause' in your contract that allows your landlord to take back the property before the end of the fixed term.

✓ You will need to have been living in the property for at least six months before a Possession Order can take effect. This means the landlord cannot force you to leave until they have obtained a court order for possession.

Anti-social behaviour

Landlords do not want to rent to people who may cause anti-social behaviour. It's added aggravation and is time-consuming to deal with. Councils certainly don't want it. They too have enough aggravation as a result of this, especially in student areas (where there are complaints of too many HMOs or the 'studentification' of an area). This means that many councils are getting tougher on miscreants.

If the neighbours complain to the council as a result of noise, violence, drug use, harassment or threats, you could end up being evicted for anti-social behaviour.

→ **At the end of the fixed term**

At the end of the fixed term, the landlord **doesn't need a reason to evict you.** As long as they have given you the correct notice (Section 21), they can apply to the court for a possession order. If they haven't completed the correct documentation then they can't evict you at the end of the agreement.

If the court gives your landlord a possession order and you still don't leave, your landlord must apply for a warrant for eviction, in which case bailiffs can be called in to remove you and your belongings from the property.

Nobody other than a bailiff acting for the county court is allowed to physically remove you from the accommodation, and should anyone else attempt to do this they may be illegally trying to evict you. If this happens you should seek immediate legal advice.

Section 21 Notice to Quit

Under the Notice to Quit procedure, the landlord will only be able to regain possession of the property at the end of the Assured Shorthold Tenancy. It is commonly known as a "Section 21" because it operates under Section 21 of the Housing Act 1988. A Possession Order using this procedure can be for any reason and is valid providing the correct legal procedure is followed.

In order to obtain possession at the end of the tenancy, the landlord must serve a written Section 21 notice on the tenant stating this intention, and since 2015 this is now only permitted after four months of the originating tenancy and it can only apply for the subsequent six months of the tenancy agreement. (This means that in an 11 month AST they cannot issue the S21 until there are six months remaining, which is month five.)

In doing this they must provide a minimum of two months' notice, although many people mistakenly believe that only a month's notice is required.

CHAPTER THIRTEEN

End of Contract

Figure 34 - Blood transfusion. Cash transference.

I referred to this earlier in the book, but it's worth asking again: do you know of any students who have NOT had money deducted from their deposit?

If you do then you are in the company of a very select few. It's as rare as someone beating Serena Williams 6-0, 6-0, an England win after the group stages of a football knockout competition, Kanye West being modest or seven days of cloudless skies across the UK.

Rant alert There is a LOT of money at stake here and frequently the blood transfusion of money to a landlord isn't prevented. This is staggering. Whilst it's understandable that many people don't understand how to challenge it or how to prepare for it (they didn't have the benefit of this book :-)), it seems that many students just don't bother. How can several hundred pounds of their or The Bank of Mum and Dad's money not be important? Or am I just a grizzly northern git who worries too much?

Before You Move

Right then, I am fizzing with ideas that can help you.

The first thing I suggest you do is phone your agent and ask if they will visit to have a look around and make suggestions as to what needs doing to minimise the chances of any part of your deposit being withheld. Then take their advice and GOWI.

Aside from their recommendations, you need to do the following:

→ **Pre-departure cleaning**

In order to get your full deposit returned you will need to clean your accommodation. It's worth emphasising…

…it will be a financial mistake not to thoroughly clean all the rooms.

Every agent and student landlord I have spoken to has told me **the biggest cause of recharges to students are made because of lack of cleaning.** It's probably because students think a house clean will take a couple of hours and maybe cost £20. So very wrong!

I have been told that 90% of student properties need a professional clean after the tenants have departed. Professional standards are much higher than you realise – it takes half a day to clean a bathroom and bedroom thoroughly. Just a kitchen on its own will take half a day. Expect to pay £200 for your house to be cleaned.

If you choose to pay for a cleaner yourself, then book them in weeks in advance because lots of students are booking cleaners at the same time. As Fred Pontin used to say in his cringeworthy TV ads, *"Book early!"*

If you sensibly choose to do the cleaning yourself then make sure you have cleaning chemicals and cloths for everyone. Soap, 'CIF', Scotch-Bright cleaning pads, glass cleaner, oven cleaner, bathroom lime scale remover, HG mould spray and bleach. However, be careful when using strong chemicals – read the instructions. The likes of bleach and the bellowing Barry Scott's Cillit Bang are powerful and can damage some surfaces.

Obviously, each of you should be responsible for your own bedroom, but…

…it's sensible that each person's bedroom is checked by someone else, because if they have fallen to temptation and cut corners you will get recharged.

Therefore, you all need to agree that nobody can leave without the rest of you being happy with the state that each room has been left in.

Here are some tips to help you along:

a) **In the kitchen,** clean the inside and outside of all cupboards, work surfaces and tiles, especially around the cooker and inside the fridge and freezer. And don't forget the floor.

b) **Oven cleaning** takes some considerable time and will take two to three attempts, even using an oven-cleaning spray. The following oven-cleaning guide may be helpful to you: www.goodhousekeeping.co.uk/lifestyle/declutter-your-home/how-to-clean-an-oven-quickly

c) **Remember to remove your own furniture** – you might think next year's students will like it, but your landlord may charge you to remove it.

d) **Clean the toilets** (squirt a toilet cleaner up inside the rim and leave it overnight – this will remove most of the stains. Then wipe around the pan, clean the seat and its underside, wipe down the WHOLE of the pan and floor, clean the basin and bath and remove hair from the plugholes (especially if there have been female tenants) – hair collects detritus and chemicals that leave an unpleasant odour. Also clean the shower screen or curtain (you will be surprised at the build-up caused by shower products).

e) **Use HG mould spray to clean tiles and silicone**. This is a professional's cleaner and is highly recommended because it requires little effort. However, you MUST follow the instructions. Do an internet search for suppliers.

f) **Don't forget the garden!**

 It's best to **prepare in advance** and get **all** your housemates involved in the cleaning. Unfortunately, it's inevitable that someone will make excuses to avoid this time-consuming chore. If someone genuinely can't make the date for your "task-force" then maybe you should agree in advance a financial compensation for those who do the work.

Organise Your Move

If you are only moving a short distance and don't have many possessions, you could move everything yourself and maybe 'employ' a couple of friends for the cost of a drink or two. However, if you have more substantial belongings, you could rent a van, although there may be age restrictions. You will be surprised at how inexpensive it can be and it certainly reduces the number of journeys that you'll have to make by car.

Sorting the bills

Before you move out you need to contact your utility service providers for gas, electricity and water and let them know you are moving out. They will need to have final meter readings, and you will need to ensure you are not liable for any additional charges after you have moved out.

The utility suppliers may wish to visit and complete the final meter reading themselves and you should also provide them with a forwarding address for the final bill (you will need this to finalise your deposit refund).

I recommend that you don't ask for the services to be disconnected, as your landlord will probably have to pay to get them reconnected and could take the cost of this out of your deposit.

So:

✓ Get readings for gas, electricity and water if you have a meter.

Make a note of these readings to ensure no future problems occur.

✓ Ask for email confirmation that you will no longer be liable for any further charges.

✓ Ensure you keep a copy of all your final bills, as your landlord or letting agent may want proof that you have paid them.

✓ In your rush, don't forget to refer to your previous bills to make sure that your final one is correct.

However, if you are on an 'all-inclusive' tenancy then you need to ensure that any charges are in line with your Agreement.

If your Agreement is one where the landlord pays for the utilities and then recharges you, be aware that the landlord CANNOT MAKE A PROFIT on utility supplies.

They can only charge you for the actual cost plus a reasonable admin fee (which may change when the planned legislation to ban letting agent fees is finally agreed). So, make sure that what you have paid tallies with the bills. It's best to ask for copies of them and also check the meter readings that have been quoted because if they are "estimated" then you may be over charged.

Redirect your post

Don't forget to write, email or text your family, friends and service providers to inform them of your new address.

To help save time, it's worth registering at www.iammoving.com, as they have a huge database of companies and can contact them free of charge.

There will always be someone you initially forget, so it may be worth contacting Royal Mail to have all your post redirected.

The day you leave

- ✓ Lock all doors and windows, including the garage.

- ✓ Make sure you have carried out any repairs you're responsible for (check your tenancy agreement if you're not sure what these are) and repair any damage you may have caused.

- ✓ Put the rubbish bags out.

- ✓ Take everything with you and don't leave things for the agent or landlord to clear out. They will recharge you.

- ✓ Make sure you return the keys to your landlord or letting agent and provide them with a forwarding address, especially in case you left something behind.

 Take detailed and dated photographs inside and outside, so you have photographic evidence of the condition you left the property in. Make sure the camera date-stamps the photos.

Deposit Refund

Your landlord must return your deposit within 10 days of the end of the AST (i.e. after you have moved out of the property), but it's likely there will be items he or she will try to make a deduction for.

The landlord simply cannot retain the deposit or any part of it without giving explicit and clear written reasons for doing so. In addition, even if they have a valid reason for withholding part of the deposit, they cannot withhold all of it. They can only withhold for a financial loss.

It is a contentious area where many students just accept the deduction because it doesn't sound like much, especially when divided amongst all the housemates. You should speak to your landlord for an explanation of why they are withholding your deposit. As students have a lack of knowledge of their legal position they are vulnerable to landlords and agents taking an aggressive stance to effectively make a profit to which they are not entitled.

So do not accept the withholding of any of the deposit without checking the facts immediately.

The best approach is to be present when the check-out inventory is being carried out, for which a time needs to be agreed with you and your housemates. Make sure you leave yourself plenty of time in order to do a thorough tidy up and repair items where you can.

a) Look back on your original photos and reposition furniture and fittings as close as possible to the original layout. Remove any stains from the carpets.

b) Make it look like you've taken care of the property – this will create a good impression even if it's just superficial. You don't want the agent or landlord feeling aggravated or appalled, as they will then start looking closely for anything they can blame and recharge you for.

c) Scuffs on the paintwork will generally come out by cleaning gently with a soapy, non-abrasive cloth, and you will be surprised how easy this is. Just don't rub too hard otherwise the emulsion paint will thin down too.

d) Replace all the items that you changed, e.g. lampshades.

e) Straighten light fittings. Remove cobwebs. Remove evidence of damp (See chapter 11).

> **When the agent, landlord or inventory clerk visit to complete the check-out inventory they should check the contents against the inventory that you signed when you first moved in.**

If (and this would be surprising) there is **no damage** and your rent is up-to-date you are entitled to your full deposit back. However, before this money is returned to you, the landlord or agent is likely to want to see proof that you have paid all your bills, so make sure you show them this before you leave. As not all of your bills will have been paid at this stage, your final meter readings need to be given to your utility providers so you can settle up ASAP. This means that some of the deposit may be held back until you have proof of payment.

If some of your deposit is held back pending proof of all bills being paid, ensure you follow up to get your refund and that you immediately inform the Deposit Scheme.

Deductions from your deposit

Your landlord can make these up to the cost of their loss if:

✓ The property has been damaged.

✓ Items are missing.

✓ The property needs to be cleaned.

✓ You left before the end of your tenancy (if you leave in accordance with your Agreement they cannot recharge you for the costs of re-letting/finding another tenant).

✓ Rent is unpaid (this is not necessarily correct in law but you will know you haven't paid, so it's better to allow this than have the landlord take you to court).

Your landlord is entitled to deduct any unpaid rent from your deposit. If you owe an amount that is greater than your deposit, he or she has the right to take court action to get a full reimbursement.

There are a couple of points that need highlighting here.

→ **Fair wear and tear**

Your landlord cannot deduct from your deposit for issues that would be as a result of "fair wear and tear," even though something may be in a worse condition than when you moved in.

"Fair wear and tear" is obviously an undefined term that is open to interpretation, so if the landlord is deducting for something that you think is fair wear and tear, put in a dispute and let the arbitrator decide.

As an example, if the carpet is showing signs of wear, it's probably as a result of general wear and tear over a number of years, but if you burn a hole in it then that is damage for which you will be liable to pay for.

The amount of wear and tear depends on:

a) The condition of the accommodation when you moved in.

b) The length of time you lived there.

If you disagree then you need to compare the check-in and check-out inventories. This is the time that having photographs in the inventory or in your own records will be a major benefit.

→ Dilapidation/damage charges

These should be itemised so that you can verify them, and this will also help you to allocate costs to individual rooms/culprits, with the communal areas separated, as they should be a shared cost.

How much can they charge?

It's always sensible to ask for quotes for any repair work or cleaning that needs doing. If you think these are excessive you can arrange to get your own ones carried out. You don't have to use the landlord's contractors. Charges for work have to be reasonable and justifiable.

Your landlord can only retain the value of repairing or replacing any damaged item 'like for like' – NOT the cost of the item brand new. They can also charge for the labour costs, e.g. for an electrician if you haven't replaced blown light bulbs.

Do check your tenancy agreement for clauses about cleaning. Some of these are reasonable while others definitely aren't. For example, they frequently state that carpets and curtains must be cleaned to a professional standard before the tenant moves out. When you consider what is "fair wear and tear" then they don't need to be as clean or cleaner than when you moved in. If the clause states the above, then as mentioned earlier in the book, you are protected by our friend The Unfair Terms in Consumer Contracts Regulations 1999.

However, irrespective of the semantics and vague legal definitions, do ensure you clean them to the best of your ability and remove any stains.

You are only required to put right any damage or clean any items that are soiled beyond what would be considered as normal wear and tear. This would include removing smells and stains/discolouration from the paintwork as a result of smoking tobacco. Keep the receipts for any work that you pay for, as these may prove to be useful in showing that work has been carried out.

Deposit disputes

If you are unable to reach an agreement over the amount of the refund, the Deposit Protection Scheme needs to become involved, so quickly get in touch with the landlord's scheme as soon as possible, as there may be a limit on the time you have to raise a dispute.

The dispute will be resolved for free via an appointed arbitrator. This is called the Alternative Dispute Resolution (ADR) and if you and the landlord both agree to use the service you will be asked to provide evidence and the resulting decision will be final.

However, this does not prevent either you or the landlord deciding to take the matter to a small claims court instead of using the ADR.

Under the custodial scheme, the disputed amount will continue to be held until the ADR or courts decide what is fair.

Under the insurance schemes, the landlord (or the agent) must hand over the disputed amount to be held until an agreement is reached. If the agent or landlord fails to do this then the scheme will pay the tenants the owed money and endeavour to get the rest back from the landlord.

→ **Deposit conditions in the tenancy agreement**

The tenancy agreement should state all the circumstances in which the deposit will be returned.

Getting your deposit back

If you think your landlord hasn't used a Tenancy Deposit Protection (TDP) scheme when they should have done, you can apply to a county court.

Get legal advice before applying to court (use the Citizens Advice Bureau).

If the court finds your landlord hasn't protected your deposit it can order the person holding the deposit to either:

a) Repay it to you.

b) Pay it into a custodial TDP scheme's bank account within 14 days.

The court may also order the landlord to pay you up to three times the deposit within 14 days of making the order.

The scheme will refund your deposit if the dispute resolution service agrees this is fair.

> If you want the full information,
> check out the following website: www.gov.uk/
> tenancy-deposit-protection/overview

If the landlord owes you money

If the landlord owes you money for any reason (e.g. you inadvertently overpaid your monthly rent) and refuses to return it, get some guidance from the Students' Union or Citizens Advice Bureau.

Ultimately, you can go to the small claims court, so if you need further information check out the following: www.gov.uk/make-court-claim-for-money/overview

Oh sh**

*"Oh sh** (choose your own appropriate expletive), I've returned the (*****y) keys but left my (****ing) mobile at the property."*

Yep, we all do it sometimes. You've left something important at the property that you've just vacated and no longer have access to.

Do not despair. The landlord cannot keep or dispose of them without following a process, and any clause in the agreement regarding this must comply with The Torts (Interference with Goods) Act 1977.

When you realise you have left something contact the landlord or agent immediately to arrange to collect it. Also, put this in writing to them.

The landlord should be aware they are not even supposed to move any items, so they should be keen for you to collect them. However, we have to be practical here, as they also need to re-rent the property, so don't delay your collection.

Conversely, if the landlord finds the items before you realise you have left them, he or she has to prove he has attempted to contact you regarding them and provide you with full contact details. He is not permitted to sell the items for a period of time after you have left. However, it's not clear how long this is. I've read it's three months, but I've had a solicitor tell me it's 14 days, so best to say one month. The tenancy agreement may state the amount of time and the Torts Act has a lot more information on this topic.

The landlord can, however, charge for his expenses in storing the item(s).

CHAPTER FOURTEEN

International Students

Figure 35 - Map of the World

International Students

This book was written with a view to helping students and their parents. When I started writing it, I hadn't even considered the international student population. It was only when I met people and businesses locally that I discovered the extent of the student population. I believe that international students number approximately 30% of all the students in the Bournemouth area (which is where I lived when I wrote most of this book).

Many of these attend the English language schools, which are commercial enterprises, and their courses can vary in length from three months upwards. This means that these students' needs are often somewhat different.

Whilst the rest of this book remains relevant to international students, it would be inappropriate for me not to provide some specific information to help them.

It's not an area where there is much information because in many countries, particularly where the student has signed up to a commercial English language course, an agent handles their UK attendance.

So, in writing for the benefit of international students, I have to assume that a reputable agent is being used and that you have selected the most suitable course and school to attend.

A lot of this chapter is about helping you research effectively and discover what questions to ask in order to lessen the chance of making mistakes. It will also help you get organised before and during your stay in the UK, which will save you a lot of time and provide you with a more enjoyable and secure experience.

Useful research for International students

 For an English language course, I recommend that the school/college is a member of English UK— www.englishuk.com/en/about-us—and accredited by the British Council, as this will ensure the highest standards.

This website is useful for choosing a university: www.ucas.com/how-it-all-works/international

It's worth checking this website for scholarships: www.educationuk.org/global/articles/higher-education-costs-scholarships/

The British Council provide a huge amount of useful information for students who are studying in the UK www.educationuk.org/global/main/living-and-studying/

Having really enjoyed living in Bournemouth, I am biased, but personally I couldn't think of a better location in the UK to learn the English language than this seaside town. This is because:

✓ The weather is at least as good as anywhere in England.

✓ There are miles of sandy beaches.

✓ There is a big student population, so it's easy to make friends.

✓ There is a good social life, with literally hundreds of restaurants, bars and hotels where you can find temporary work (visa rules permitting) and meet people to learn the language every day.

✓ The locals do not have a pronounced regional accent, so they are easier to understand.

Accommodation

As an international student, you have the added complication of finding accommodation before you arrive in the UK. (Refer to the principles concerning location and where to look outlined in Chapter 3 'Leaving Home'.

It's worth asking your university/college/school if there is a guarantee of accommodation for new international students for their first year and for any subsequent years of study. Also check whether there is a deadline for submitting your application.

In addition, if you have to organise your own accommodation, I recommend that you don't rent a property until you have seen it, and certainly don't send money to anyone as a deposit.

As already outlined in this book, there has been an increase in the number of frauds where people are advertising properties they do not own, so if you are not careful your deposit could get stolen.

If you are having to organise your own accommodation rather than going into halls, arrange to spend your first few nights in a hostel, guesthouse or with a homestay family close to the college. This will allow you time to meet people and get to know the area. You'll then be able to choose an appropriate location and accommodation that is within your budget. Perhaps you will also find a trustworthy person to share with.

In doing your search for accommodation, all the previous chapters are relevant.

Another alternative if you are attending a language school is to ask if they have any families registered who are looking to provide accommodation for students. Most will have a good selection of families and the school will try to find one that matches your requirements.

Students can integrate with these families as a lodger, which will also help them improve their English.

Figure 36 - What questions to ask?

To understand what is included in the cost of the accommodation, you'll need to ask the following questions:

- ✓ Are the following included: meals, utility bills (gas, electricity and water)? What's the approximate cost of these each month?

- ✓ Does the price include contents insurance?

- ✓ Is there broadband in the accommodation? If so, is there an extra cost or limit on the usage?

- ✓ Are bed linen, towels and kitchen utensils provided? If not, does the institution offer packs I can buy?

- ✓ Will council tax need to be paid? If so, how much?

- ✓ For car users, are there parking facilities? If so, is there an extra cost?

- ✓ Is a deposit required? If so, how much is it?

- ✓ How should payments be made?

- ✓ Is there a communal living space? If so, how many people will be using it?

- ✓ Is the bathroom an en-suite or shared?

- ✓ What space will be allocated for food storage?

- ✓ What's the length of the rental contract?

What to bring to the UK:

- ✓ Passport – ensure that it will be valid for the full length of your stay.

    Depending upon your country of origin you may need a visa. It's advisable to apply for this well in advance of your journey to the UK. As with your passport, ensure it remains valid throughout your stay. See: www.ukba.homeoffice.gov.uk/visas-immigration/do-you-need-a-visa/

✓ Mobile or smartphone. Additionally, it may be cheaper for you to buy a UK SIM card.

✓ Driving licence.

✓ Proof of identity.

✓ Electrical socket adaptors.

✓ Battery chargers.

✓ Laptop or computing device with Internet and Wi-Fi connection for the UK.

✓ Software downloaded and prepared, e.g. Skype. Ensure close friends and relatives also have Skype accounts so you can keep in closer contact.

✓ List of your internet passwords.

✓ Sufficient Cash in £ sterling for two days.

✓ A pre-paid cash card that you can use anywhere you see the MasterCard sign.

✓ A print out of all your personal contacts in case your mobile phone gets damaged or lost.

✓ Telephone numbers and addresses you will need in the UK.

Also

✓ Open a bank account before your arrival, preferably one that offers internet banking and both a debit card and credit card.

✓ Ensure you can transfer money easily and securely.

✓ If your VISA status allows it, get a UK National Insurance number so you can work without paying additional tax. Then enquire how you can claim back any tax you have overpaid.

✓ Remember to give your friends and relatives your address in the UK and send them a message once you arrive at your destination.

✓ You may also want to arrange health cover whilst in the UK or perhaps travelling around Europe too. Take a look at this website: www.nhs.uk/nhsengland/Healthcareabroad/Pages/Healthcareabro ad.aspx

✓ If you are planning to rent a property or even share a rented property as your main home, your landlord will be required to make checks to comply with the 'Right to Rent' legislation. This means they will need to see the originals of your proof of identity and your visa, if you have one. It's therefore important to ensure that these documents are in good condition before you leave for the UK and that they are kept in good condition once you have arrived.

After arrival

Figure 37 - What is this? What am I supposed to do?

✓ Get to know your location and how to travel to your school/college/university.

✓ Find the local supermarket and buy some food and other supplies, e.g. toothpaste and brush, soap, etc.

✓ Learn how to use cash machines (ATM).

✓ Write down emergency telephone numbers and keep these with you.

✓ Get familiar with safety rules for using roads, whether you are driving, cycling or walking.

✓ Make sure you understand personal security issues. Many of these are common sense but some may be different in the UK to those you are familiar with at home.

✓ To help you, I have added Appendix 2, which relates to security issues.

Socialising

✓ If attending university, become a member of the Students' Union.

✓ Research sports and social clubs that might be of interest to you, as well as activities that your school or college organises.

✓ Get a map so you can mark where there are places of interest.

✓ Get to understand the local culture, when people go out and where they go.

Council tax

For council tax payments, the following are not noted as adults, and so are exempt from payments:

✓ Children under 18; people on apprenticeships.

✓ 18 and 19 year olds in full-time education, full-time college and university students, young people under 25 who get funding from the Skills Funding Agency or the Young People's Learning Agency, student nurses, foreign language assistants registered with the British Council, people with a severe mental disability and live-in carers who look after someone who isn't their partner, spouse or child.

✓ There is exemption from council tax if everyone in the house is a full-time student on a course lasting at least a year that involves 21-hours of study per week or more.

✓ Diplomats.

CONCLUSION

Some of the content of this book has been detailed, technical and maybe not so easy to follow, but if you've managed to read this far, congratulations for your persistence and determination to learn. If you haven't yet read the entire book then I hope you find it useful as a reference in the next couple of years as a student, and when the day comes when you want to rent a property and progress with your life post university.

I know that if you take the contents of this book on board you will be well prepared for dealing with the commercial world of property rentals rather than simply being an enthusiastic, smart kid with a bullseye printed on your T-shirt. You will have "armour and ammunition".

If you save money as a result of this book, and you are better able to cope with living away from home, then I will be delighted. All my time and effort will have been worth it.

It has taken over three years to get this book to publication because writing it and understanding the hidden world of publishing is difficult to fit in with a business. However, it's fun to eventually get to the finish line and it has been a tremendous learning experience. Throughout your life, I strongly recommend that you continually look for learning experiences. It's exciting, interesting and energising. I hope that you will still be fizzing even when you reach my age!

I've covered the planning of your choice of home and the commercial side of renting a property: from understanding the main players in the marketplace and searching for a suitable property, to successful ways to handle agents and landlords, as well as the documentation, the loopholes you could face and the legal requirements.

I then moved onto aspects relating to living in the property that will save you money and reduce hassle, and I looked at how to fix or resolve many issues with which you are unlikely to have had previous experience.

After this I covered preparing for leaving and the all-important aspects of getting your deposit refunded.

Finally, I examined what happens next and your future.

> There are checklists and information to make your life easier that are available to be downloaded by buyers of this book. Here you can download useful web site hyperlinks, bonus information and tips on personal development subjects that will not be available from the 'freebie' website referred to on the back cover.
> So, for these bonus downloads, go to;
> **www.smartstudentguides.com/bookdocs**

You will need to **register and create a password** because I obviously don't want everybody downloading the information, which you had the foresight to invest in, for free.

So, my thanks for reading! If you enjoyed this book or found it useful I'd be very grateful if you'd post a short review on Amazon. Your support, feedback and interest really does make a difference and I will read all the reviews so I can make this book even better.

If you discover that I've made any omissions or even mistakes, then please let me know and I will arrange updates for future publications.

If this book has helped you then I would love to hear how. It will be great to know that my effort has had a specific impact. We all need reassurance, so please let me know by email to: im@smartstudentguides.com

A Final, SMART Note

I hope that self-educating will continue as a perpetual ambition for you - it's the education that will be more important than your qualifications, so over the page are a few relevant quotes.

The important thing is not to stop questioning.
- Albert Einstein

Don't assume that your academic abilities will lead to success;
Many highly intelligent people are poor thinkers. Many people of
average intelligence are skilled thinkers. The power of the car is
separate from the way the car is driven.
- Edward De Bono

This one always makes me smile:

It's what you learn after you know it all that counts.
-John Wooden

These quotes were given to me as a young manager when I was being trained in interviewing skills, but they are so relevant to acquiring more knowledge and understanding. I just wish I had applied them more!

The quality of any answer is in inverse proportion to the length
of the question.
-Training Manager

I keep six honest serving men (they taught me all I knew);
Theirs names are What and Why and When And How
And Where and Who.
-Rudyard Kipling

I came across the information over the page just before publishing this book. I think it's brilliant because it condenses the question of how to live life into three steps and deflects us away from so-called 'stuffocation.' This is your opportunity to ask yourself SMART questions about how you will act on this crucial advice, it will make you think more about a work/life balance #suffocation

Professor Sonja Lyubomirsky (professor in the Department of Psychology at the University of California) says that the problem with buying 'stuff' is that the happiness resulting from it is relatively short lived.

This provides a strong contrast to experiences, which create much longer lasting and happier memories.

Her advice for making happiness last (to avoid what she refers to as 'hedonic adaptation' and the superficiality of consumerism), is to focus on having three things:

1. Great relationships, which include at least one or two very close relationships.

2. A purpose in life that drives you to get out of bed each day and make a difference.

3. A variety of peak experiences that make your heart sing. This could be anything from singing to skydiving, cooking to kung fu. It's really whatever works for you.

I couldn't agree more, so I wish you all success in finding your purpose, great relationships and experiences.

Don't forget to download your free checklists to help you:

✓ Ask pre-viewing questions.

✓ View and assess a property, so that you don't have ongoing problems.

✓ Move in with minimal stress.

✓ Understand the rules of the house.

Find all the useful websites that are referred to throughout this book by going to:

 www.smartstudentguides.com/bookdocs

FUTURE STRIDES

(OR, IN OTHER WORDS...WHAT'S NEXT?)

From SMART Student to Working SMART

Beyond university, what is the next step for a SMART student? Travel? Work? Setting up a business?

The world of employment, careers and the need to earn money can appear very daunting, especially in these current times when many graduates struggle to get the type of job they were expecting.

In this chapter I'll outline some important considerations that I hope will provoke you to invest some time into thinking about the direction to take your working life.

Everyone is a genius. By that I mean we all have some specialised skill; something we find easy, so easy we don't realise it's a skill until we notice other people find it very difficult. In sport, they tend to have a natural grace and an ability to make it look easy, instinctive, balanced and elegant (David Gower at cricket, Jeremy Guscott at rugby, George Best at football, Roger Federer at tennis, Mo Farah at running. Although I suspect you may only be familiar with two of these, you get the picture and will think of your own favourites). Some people find their talent very quickly in life, but most of us either don't realise we have it, don't look for it, or discover it late in life.

At the earliest stage, I recommend that you try to discover what your own genius is. It usually involves what you REALLY enjoy doing, so it's worth spending time reflecting on what experiences you have enjoyed most, and then writing these down. It may mean nothing to you right now, but it's important if you are going to find your genius. To help you, I recommend you do some psychometric tests to at least give you a bit of direction.

Your working life is not a fixed trajectory. At some stage it will go off course, but at all times it is YOU who is in control of the settings, so you will need to take active measures to navigate around obstacles and widen your learning so you can continue your journey. Take some thinking time. Give some thought to how the world will evolve. This is important for all of us. The speed of scientific and technological advances is absolutely amazing but the rate of change will continue to increase. None of us can afford to stop learning. University is a just a start for the smart.

As technology progresses, jobs will rapidly evolve and many will disappear. This is referred to as "creative destruction". For example, what will happen to taxi drivers, bus drivers, train drivers (if you commute using Southern Rail you probably can't wait for driverless trains and the marginalising of unions!), car ownerships, factory workers, retail jobs? Will German car manufacturers still dominate, which, therefore, also means German manufacturing? How will speech recognition software affect employment and consumer goods when everything will be linked through the "Internet of Things" using "Big Data"?

These are obvious changes, but less so are solicitors. What will happen when search engines can research legal case histories within minutes, and conveyancing information on properties will be available on a single database and also substantially reduce property transaction times? (I bet you didn't know that a property sale from offer to completion can happen in 24 hours even now!).

What about education and universities, when an increasing amount of courses and corporate and small business training will be completed online? It will certainly create more opportunities for people in IT and those with communication, organising, studio filming and audio skills.

What will happen when average life expectancy is 100 years? When will people retire? How will pensions be paid? How will we accommodate the need for more medical attention and care homes?

In the property industry, can you see plumbers and electricians being replaced by robots? Certainly not until they replace all the current housing stock (is that likely within three generations?). There is a lot of competition, albeit mediocre, so the task is, as with all industries, to deliver a higher-quality experience for customers. Charlie Mullins, the founder of Pimlico Plumbers, wrote a book called Bog-Standard Business detailing how he built a massively successful business mainly as a result of his attention to detail and despite charging fees that are way in excess of his competitors. Everyone needs to find a competitive edge.

Economics, finance and politics have a massive impact on us all, so it will give you a massive advantage to understand them and get ahead of the herd. They may not have much appeal but you will find it heartening that just a superficial understanding of economics will put you ahead of most of the population (including politicians!). You will then be able to ask smarter questions and make your own judgements. This will mean you won't have to rely on the media (which always has an agenda).

In the future, many people will have portfolio careers, meaning they will have several jobs or sources of income. There will certainly be more freelancers and more people working remotely, which could be from another country.

Whatever your source of income, you will have competition. This means that you will need to make yourself more marketable and be able to present and project a good image of yourself both in written form and face-to-face. Whatever you do, you will do it better with good marketing skills.

It would be useful to spend some time getting advice on preparing your CV and how to tailor-make applications. Speak to HR professionals as well as careers advisers in education, because they will have unique insights. Once you get to an interview, there are additional skills to master. Having the best degree from the best university will get you a long way, but take heart if you didn't get a first, as there are other skills that will really help you to compete. A CV only gets you an interview. Interviewers will assess you to see how you will fit into the culture of the company and this will include how you will get on with your co-workers and help the company move in its desired direction.

It took me far too many years to learn (or maybe I never learned) that in corporate life your job is usually to make your boss look good, rather than to make the company more efficient, productive or profitable. If you have a high EQ (Emotional Intelligence) as well as a high IQ, you have more than a head start. Your ability to get on with people will be a major factor in your future success. In fact, I now believe that EQ is more important than IQ.

The great news is that EQ can be learned, so it's well worth doing some research, reading or even completing an e-learning programme.

Educating the mind without educating the heart
is no education at all.
- Aristotle

Now, having prompted you to think about your future career, you might want to start acquiring some skills that will be immediately useful: speed reading and mind mapping could be very helpful whilst you are at university.

Some topics for you to consider are:

✓ Job applications and CVs

✓ Interviews

✓ Career planning

- ✓ Psychometric tests
- ✓ Time management
- ✓ Speed reading
- ✓ Presentations
- ✓ Mind mapping
- ✓ NLP
- ✓ Body language and personal projection
- ✓ Health, fitness and diet

These topics can be very detailed and scientifically technical (even the last one), as they are primarily aimed at trainers, consultants and academics rather than providing quick tips for self-development.

> If you would like recommendations, do please email me at
> **im@smartstudentguides.com**
> and state which topic interests you.

Additionally, moving on to the specifics of my main business, which is property investing, rentals and management, I plan to add to the website a dictionary of terminology that I have prepared and also provide property-related advice.

So if these areas interest you, then similarly please email me at im@smartstudentguides.com and let me know what you would like to learn more about.

APPENDIX 1

Tenancies in Scotland

As a quick reminder, laws relating to property are currently changing regularly, and in Scotland they are even more focused on benefiting the tenant, so please use this section as a guide and do your own research in order to get the most up-to-date information before committing to anything.

In Scotland, a tenant is most likely to be offered a Short Assured Tenancy governed by the Housing (Scotland) Act 1988. There are certain requirements that a landlord must meet to ensure he sets up a Short Assured Tenancy. If he fails to do that the position would be covered by the Rent (Scotland) Act 1984, which could lead to the tenancy being a "protected" one and make it difficult for the landlord to recover possession of the property.

> **For a landlord to let out property, he must be registered with the local authority as a private landlord. A landlord should let the tenant have a note of his registration number at the beginning of the tenancy.**

It is a criminal offence to let out the property for residential use in the private sector unless the landlord has been registered with their local authority.

An Energy Performance Certificate is required when a property is rented out to tenants and the EPC must be made available free of charge to a prospective tenant at the time they request information about the property or make a request to view it.

The local authority is responsible for enforcing these requirements and can request the production of the EPC for inspection. A penalty can be imposed if the landlord has breached his duty.

There are duties imposed on private sector landlords in relation to the Repairing Standards for the property. These require the landlord to carry out a pre-tenancy inspection of the house to identify any work required to meet the Repairing Standards, and the landlord is required to notify the tenant if any such work is needed.

It is recommended for the landlord to send a letter to the tenants with regard to the Repairing Standard and whether any works are required to be carried out.

There are other responsibilities placed on landlords in terms of gas safety, electrical testing and other matters that relate to the property for which local authorities usually produce guidance. For a tenant, it is worth getting a copy of these.

When the landlord has complied with these duties he should offer the tenant the lease, which should include the basic information of the address of the property, the term of the lease (a Short Assured Tenancy must be for at least six months) and the rent payable. The landlord is also required to provide the tenant with notice of a Short Assured Tenancy, and this is done by way of Form AT5, which usually accompanies the lease provided by the landlord.

A Tenant Information Pack must also be issued to every tenant and if the tenancy is a joint one each individual tenant must receive a separate pack.

For information on tenant packs visit:
www.scotland.gov.uk/
Publications/2013/02/8719/downloads

If the property has gas supplied then the tenant should be provided with a copy of a Gas Safety Certificate.

If a deposit is required and is received by the landlord he must comply with the Tenancy Deposit Scheme (Scotland) Regulations 2011.

The landlord must pay the deposit into an approved scheme and he or she must ensure that the monies are held in this scheme for the duration of the tenancy.

Three schemes have been approved in Scotland. These are:

1. Letting Protection Service Scotland

2. SafeDeposits, Scotland

3. My Deposits Scotland

The Unfair Contract Terms Act also applies in Scotland, as does the Property Misdescriptions Act.

The liability for hazards in a property are normally governed by The Occupiers' Liability (Scotland) Act 1960.

Generally, a landlord has the right to inspect the property upon giving reasonable notice to a tenant and that applies whether or not it is specifically mentioned in the lease itself.

To regain possession, the landlord must serve the tenant with a Notice to Quit. Section 33 of the Housing (Scotland) Act 1988 applies.

The landlord must give at least two months' notice, and the notice should state that the landlord wishes to recover possession of the property.

It is not essential for the landlord to serve an AT6 Form along with the Notice to Quit, but the two are usually served at the same time.

A landlord may seek to recover possession of the property in the event of the tenant being in breach of tenancy conditions. In that case, two weeks' notice is all that is required and this notice must be accompanied by a Form AT6 specifying the grounds upon which the landlord intends to use in order to recover possession.

At the end of the period of notice, if the tenant does not vacate the property an action has to be raised which is usually by way of a Summary Cause at the local sheriff court. In the event of the landlord obtaining a Decree for Ejection, he will usually instruct sheriff officers to serve a Charge on the Tenant following on from the Decree. If the Tenant still does not leave the property, sheriff officers can be instructed to carry out an ejection.

Should the tenant vacate the property but leave some of his belongings, the landlord has a duty of "reasonable" care of those belongings. However, if the tenant does not contact the landlord within a reasonable time to recover his belongings the landlord can take steps to remove the belongings from the property.

If there is more than one tenant they are jointly liable for the rent.

It is fairly common (especially when students are the tenants of a property) for landlords to seek a guarantee or guarantees from parents. Usually each parent will be responsible for all of the rent.

Letting agents are not entitled to charge any fee for their service to the tenant, so they cannot charge the tenant for registering them nor for finding them a property to rent (in my opinion this is good for tenants but harsh on landlords, as tenants can delay completing the documentation and then pull out, thus potentially wasting a month's time and rent. To get around this, a non-refundable deposit, even if it's only £100, should be allowed).

There are no separate water bills in Scotland. These are paid as a proportion of the council tax.

If a landlord refuses to carry out repairs that he is obliged to carry out, the tenant can withhold rent and use it to carry out the repairs.

A landlord can raise an Action for Ejection at any time after the lease has commenced. This would normally only be when there have been serious breaches of the Tenancy Conditions. There are certain mandatory grounds where the court must allow the landlord to recover possession, one of those being three months' arrears of rent both at the time of the Notice to Quit being served on the tenant and at the date of the raising of the Ejection Action.

Proof of ownership

In Scotland, there is a bit more of a defence against third parties illegally renting out a property as…

it is unlawful for someone to rent a property as a landlord unless the local authority has approved of that person.

Surprisingly, this is because the Antisocial Behaviour etc. (Scotland) Act 2004 requires all landlords to be registered, so the landlord should be traceable and have a history with the local authority.

If you need to do some research, the following websites provide valuable information:

✓ www.scotland.gov.uk/topics/built-environment/ housing/privaterent/landlords/

✓ www.scotland.gov.uk/Topics/built-environment/ housing/privaterent/tenants

✓ www.homelettings.co/landlords/legal-stuf/

✓ www.rentingscotland.org/landlords-guide/starting-tenancy-landlord

Whilst the information is provided for landlords, it confirms some of the standards they should be achieving on the property that you are renting.

This one covers some specific information for tenants:

✓ www.rentingscotland.org/articles/repairing-standard

APPENDIX 2

Personal Security

This may be an issue that you haven't previously had to consider whilst living at home. Conversely, it may be one that is already of great concern to you, perhaps because of what you have read in the media.

It's all too easy to overlook or forget to check things, believing that the chance of anything happening to you is remote. Security is not just about personal safety for women. Amongst other things, it involves theft of your belongings and identity theft.

The first point you should be aware of is that your Students' Union can provide you with advice about the local area, so make contact with them during your search for accommodation. They can recommend areas to avoid. Bear in mind that some areas look fine during the day but at night they transform into something less appealing.

Personal safety

In 1986, a 25-year-old estate agent disappeared whilst meeting an unknown prospective client. Sadly, it has still not been established what happened to her. At the time this was a major news item around the country. For those of us involved in estate agency it was a terrible shock, as the young woman was doing what many agents were doing on a daily basis.

The woman's name was Suzy Lamplugh and in researching this section, I referred to the Suzy Lamplugh Trust's website. They provide education and support to help people reduce the risks of aggression and violence. Having read it, it's very informative and relevant for all students. Their website even has a section on student safety, so, with their permission, I have simply copied their content.

> If you would like to know more about the trust or about safety, their website is at www.suzylamplugh.org/Pages/FAQs/Category/personal-safety

Their content is targeted at ladies, but the principles should be noted by everyone.

The risk of suffering from violence or aggression is thankfully very low but you do need to be careful, especially when you are in a new environment with new people.

By taking some simple, basic precautions you can easily reduce the risks and take control of your own safety.

Accommodation

✓ When you leave your room in halls, always **lock the door and shut the window, even if you are only popping next door for a minute, and don't forget to switch off electrical appliances, as they are a fire risk.** Hair straighteners are the biggest problem as it's not obvious when they are switched on.

✓ Think about the risks before inviting someone you've just met into your room.

✓ Never let anyone into your block by holding a door open unless you know them or have checked their ID.

✓ If you see anything suspicious, **report it to your campus security.** It may be nothing to worry about but it's better to be safe than sorry.

✓ When choosing where to stay, **make sure it's secure and that the area feels safe.**

✓ It's a good idea to visit potential accommodation at night as well as during the day.

✓ Make sure you meet all your prospective flatmates and trust your instincts when deciding whether or not to move in.

Going out at night

Obviously for young ladies, until you know the area and you have established friendships, it's recommended that you let someone know where you are going, who you are meeting and when you expect to return. This is especially the case if you plan to have more than a couple of drinks. Plan how you are going to get home. (It's not much fun when the next train, tube or bus home is at 5:30 in the morning, you can't find a taxi and you are faced with a three-mile, inebriated walk home).

Remember, the most common date-rape drug is alcohol (by getting inebriated), so keep an eye on your drinks so they aren't surreptitiously topped-up with potent chasers or spiked with other chemicals such as date rape drugs.

Dates are safer and easier to leave quickly if they are in a public place, especially during daylight hours.

Safety when out and about

Stay Alert. If you are chatting on your mobile phone or listening to music on your headphones, you are unlikely to be aware of your surroundings and could therefore fail to notice any potential danger signs.

You may often be laden with books and bags but always try to keep one hand free and walk confidently and purposefully.

Think about getting a personal safety alarm. Keep it in an easily accessible place.

If you are out at night, try to stick to busy streets where there are other people. Try to think in advance and anticipate the danger spots, such as poorly-lit areas, deserted parks or quiet alleyways.

Face oncoming traffic when you are walking so you can more easily see dangers, and keep any bags, especially ones containing computers, on the inside so mobile bag snatchers (on bikes or through car windows) won't be so easily tempted.

Ask if there are any areas near your halls that should be avoided. Some shortcuts may be great during the day but have a reputation amongst other students for being unsafe at night.

If you see someone else in trouble, think twice before trying to help. This may just aggravate the problem and you could put yourself at risk. It may be a lot more helpful to call the police or make a lot of noise to attract attention.

If a bus is empty or it's after dark, it's better to stay on the lower deck and sit near the driver or conductor. On trains or the underground, try to sit with other people and avoid empty carriages.

Always carry the telephone numbers of a couple of trusted friends and a licensed taxi or minicab company with you on a piece of paper in case your mobile's battery goes flat, and have a suitable booking app available on your phone.

Try to avoid unlicensed minicabs, as these are unchecked, uninsured and can potentially be dangerous if you are alone.

As an additional point from me, I believe that women should carry personal alarms. However, although pepper sprays are legal in a number of other countries, they are not permitted in the UK.

Weapons of any description that are designed or adapted for the discharge of any noxious liquid, gas or other substance are prohibited.

Fraud and internet crime

Action Fraud is the UK's national reporting centre for fraud and internet crime, so you can find more details on their website: www.actionfraud.police.uk/fraud_protection/identity_fraud.

Here is some information about the different forms of internet crime and fraud:

→ **Identity theft**

This can result in people using your identity in order to fraudulently purchase goods. This can impact on your personal finances and could also adversely affect your ability to obtain credit or loans, including credit cards or even a telephone contract.

In order to protect yourself, it's advisable to do the following:

✗ Don't throw out anything with your name, address or financial details without shredding it first. If you don't have a shredder, just rip out your name and address and shred these details at uni, or rip them up and dispose of them at a different location

✗ Don't leave bills or private details lying around, even in your accommodation.

✗ If you receive an unsolicited email or phone call from what appears to be your bank or building society asking for your security details, DO NOT reveal your password, login details or account numbers. Banks will not ask directly or through a link to a webpage for your PIN or for an entire security number or password.

✗ Similarly, if you are not expecting a phone call from a bank, do not even confirm your identity over the phone. When I receive these calls I ask the caller to prove where they are from by asking them for some of my security answers in order to verify this. I recommend that you ask for the name and department of the caller, plus their phone and extension number. Use the internet to check the phone number, or the number provided on your statements and call them back on this number, not the one the caller has stated.

x   When setting up accounts with the likes of utility companies and subscriptions, I recommend avoiding giving your real date of birth or your mother's maiden name. However, with banks it's important to provide the correct information.

x   Many suppliers and local authorities now ask for your mobile phone number or email address. I recommend that you ask them why they need this because there's no reason to contact you other than via your home address. Authorities (forms of government) do not have a good record of keeping data secure (and rather disgracefully they sell some of it to marketing companies), so the less they know the better.

x   If you move address, get Royal Mail to redirect your post. I advise this for a six-month period if you can quickly inform ALL of your friends, family, banks and insurance suppliers of your change. One year is better but it's a bit more expensive.

Crime prevention, safer homes, fire safety and mobile and internet safety

There is a lot of information on this useful Neighbourhood Watch website. In fact, there is too much to simply copy and paste, so either go to the website at: www.ourwatch.org.uk/safety_advice, or download their excellent 'Stay Safe' PDF, which covers everything from their webpages that you'll need to know about safety:www.ourwatch.org.uk/uploads/pub_res/SACP_booklet_FINAL_compressed2.pdf

ABOUT THE AUTHOR

Ian Muir was brought up in Sale, Greater Manchester and has subsequently lived in a number of locations, writing this book whilst living in Bournemouth and seeing it published on his return to Surrey.

He has been refurbishing properties for renting out since 2003, originally doing most of the interior refurbishment work himself at weekends and in the evenings.

An experienced landlord both in the UK and Spain, he has a broad range of commercial experience and has seen dramatic changes in the property market with interest rates from 15% at the peak - which resulted in him being forced to sell his marital home, to today's level of 0.25% that has encouraged many people to invest in properties.

Ian came to property after a corporate background in finance and logistics, and also a period as a Training Director within a national estate agency, where he designed and ran sales and management skills training courses. However he will tell you that he wishes he'd had the foresight to have become the 'Money Saving Expert' as he has an instinct for understanding businesses, spotting obfuscation and unfair practices and finding better solutions.

His interests include personal development, current affairs, and trying to make sense of economics and politics. Socially he loves to share cooking duties over a bottle (or two) of wine, travelling to new places, and listening to a wide range of music, from Karl Jenkins' 'Armed Man' to his favourite, jazz 'fusion' and the likes of the super-talented Snarky Puppy.

He is a former competitive club cricketer and coach, although he can still be persuaded to turn out to play sport, especially tennis, the occasional golf day and lycra-free cycling.

He has just completed work on property projects in Sussex, where, following a divorce, he also enjoys spending time with his 'family' (his lovely daughter and her cats).

ACKNOWLEDGEMENTS

The book has been a 'labour of love' and certainly it would not have reached publication without the help of a number of invaluable contributions that deserve mentioning.

So, my eternal gratitude to my lovely daughter's mother, Christina, who had to tolerate my economic and political ranting and my frustration at working for other people whilst we were married.

My big thank you;

To the patient Alexa and her team at The Book Refinery – for their professional proof-reading, editing, help with the cover design and most importantly for getting me 'over the line'. You were outstanding to work with!

To David Stock at the Students' Union in Bournemouth who spared the time to give me greater understanding of the issues they, and the students, face and for his positive response to my outline of the contents.

To the expert landlady, Mary Latham, for taking the time to read my manuscript and update me on a number of impending legislation changes.

To the freelancers for their good work in producing illustrations, logos, and icons.

To my dear friend and property investor, Sara Worth for her questioning of my occasionally obtuse and regularly disjointed writings before I passed the manuscript to Alexa.

To manufacturers who have allowed me to use photographs of their products (Philips for lighting, Scolmore Group for electrical sockets, McAlpine Plumbing for waste traps, and Numatic for their vacuum cleaner) and the Suzy Lamplugh Trust for allowing me to copy content from their website.

To David Jones, from the ETC International College, for his suggestions on improving the clarity of the chapter for international students and for his schoolmasterly, red ink correcting of my grammar. And, most importantly, for completing the onerous task of writing the foreword to the book.

My special thanks go to the excellent Ian Grant of Smiths Grant Solicitors in Duns, Scottish Borders (who I have been using for property-related legal work in Scotland), for taking the time to prepare the Scottish content in the Appendix free of charge (so this disproves the saying that a Scotsman is like a Yorkshireman with all the generosity squeezed out of them).

An additional note of thanks to politicians and economists, who normally get berated by me but whose selective (mis)use of statistics taught me the need to improve the key skills of numeracy and of asking smarter questions.

As my book is aimed at university students, here are some quotes on the subject of education ...

"I can only say that I view it as the most important subject which we as a people may be engaged in."
- Abraham Lincoln

"Education is what remains after one has forgotten what one has learned in school."
- Albert Einstein

"If a man empties his purse into his head, no man can take it away from him. An investment in knowledge always pays the best interest."
- Ben Franklin

"Self-education is, I firmly believe, the only kind of education there is."

- Isaac Asimov

"If you want happiness for a lifetime, help the next generation."

- Chinese proverb

Thank you for buying this book and for investing in my 'university of life' knowledge for your self-education. May your investment pay large, compounding dividends.

Don't forget to download the **FREE CHECKLISTS**, useful web site hyperlinks and bonus information to make your life easier. Go to:

www.smartstudentguides.com/bookdocs